Dorothy Larsen

A Touch Of Sage

Reflections on growth, change, and growing older

CompCare® Publishers
2415 Annapolis Lane
Minneapolis, Minnesota 55441

Library of Congress Cataloging-in-Publication Data
Larsen, Dorothy, 1915–
A touch of sage

Includes index.
1. Old Age—Quotations, maxims, etc.   2. Life—Quotations,
maxims, etc.   I. Title.
PN6084.05L3 1989   818'.5402   89-9929
ISBN 0-89638-170-6

Cover and interior design by Lillian Svec

Inquiries, orders, and catalog requests should be addressed to
CompCare Publishers
2415 Annapolis Lane
Minneapolis, Minnesota 55441
Call toll free 800/328-3330
(Minnesota residents 612/559-4800)

5	4	3	2	1
93	92	91	90	89

This book is dedicated to those now living the last quarter of their lives with honesty, humor, hope, and heroism.

I also dedicate this book to my dear children — Katie, Carol, Earnie, Steve, and Bill — all now grown into productive and wonderful human beings. Without their interest and encouragement, this book would have never been completed.

OUR BASIC RIGHTS

1. The right to be treated with respect.
2. The right to fulfill our needs.
3. The right to love and be loved.
4. The right to happiness.
5. The right to give as well as receive.
6. The right to security.
7. The right to joy and laughter.
8. The right to play.
9. The right to maintain meaningful relationships.
10. The right to express our feelings.
11. The right to be listened to and taken seriously.
12. The right to disagree.
13. The right to privacy.
14. The right to ask questions.
15. The right to be ourselves, the way we are, the way we want to be.

Contents

Introduction: The State of the Art of Growing Old

Introduction: The State of the Art of Growing Old

The expression *state of the art* is very much in use these days. State of the art in medicine, in computers, in outer space exploration, in all facets of our lives. The state of the art of growing old in the last part of the twentieth century is of no less interest, at least to us "over sixty-fivers."

Retirees are receiving more attention and consideration today, thanks in part to our growing numbers. The Census Bureau says that in 1900 only one American in twenty-five was over sixty-five. It projects that by the middle of the next century one American in four will be sixty-five or older. During this century we gained twenty-six years of life expectancy. This is nearly equal to what mankind gained in the preceding five thousand years. Also, our impact at the cash register has caught the attention of the marketplace. And more and more of us are exercising, participating in sports, remaining active in the work force and in politics. We are taking charge of our individual health care, living habits, and environment. The fact that life expectancy is rising proves this point.

Yes, the state of the art of growing old at the end of the twentieth century is alive and holds much promise. The odds for a better, healthier, and longer life are improving all the time.

Courage

Often the test of courage is to live.
Anyone can die.

Vittorio Alfieri

So many happenings throughout the days and years call for courage. The weak-hearted fall by the wayside; the courageous make it to the top.

A news commentator was closing his broadcast with the word, "Courage!" The public hooted it down. Such an obvious lack of introspection and unwillingness to accept reality is hard to understand. We should not only be courageous, but know and understand why we are, and what we are courageous about. The only way to serenity in this life is through courageous action and acceptance. It is required of us at every turn—courage to speak out, courage to persevere through pain, courage to persist in a good health regimen, courage to resist defeat.

Why let our courage flag and be afraid of tomorrow? We have seen yesterday and conquered it. Today we choose to live courageously. Winston Churchill was right when he said: "Courage is the first of human qualities because it is the quality which guarantees all the rest."

Imagination

Imagination, the elixir of life!
P. T. Barnum

Some of us are more creative, more imaginative, than others. It comes about from not always following the beaten path, from letting our originality take over.

With practice, we can get into the knack of allowing ourselves to escape the humdrum routine, just as we did when we were children. A few flights of fancy are not only harmless, but rejuvenating. A little castle-building never hurt anyone. Imagination can be utilized beneficially in practically all facets of our lives. We can use imagination in mundane activities such as decorating, cooking, dressing, letter-writing, conversations, gardening, recreation, etc. Encourage fertile and inventive thoughts.

Cervantes' Don Quixote spoke of dreaming the impossible dream and reaching the unreachable star. That can never happen without imagination to set the goal and give the impetus. Imagine how dull our lives would be without imagination!

Joy

*Real joy comes not from ease or riches or
the praise of men, but from doing
something worthwhile.*

W. T. Granfell

Joy can be experienced in various degrees of intensity, from gaiety to a deep sense of well-being that fosters peace and serenity. Visits from our children and grandchildren, the return of the birds in spring, the first early blossoms, happy times spent with friends, and pleasant surprises are so welcome because they bring us joy and pleasure.

There is also the deeper level of joy—an inner spiritual joy. The Bible says that the Spirit brings love, joy, and peace. It gives us an inner strength that no one can take away from us. The secret of true joy is putting others first and abandoning selfishness. Only then will we find true peace and joy. Peace and joy should be our goals. Whatever we do, we should be striving for that. There isn't any formula; we learn joy by living a joyous life.

Choices

*When you have to make a choice and
don't make it, that is a choice.*

William James

Regardless of what has happened to us in the past, we need not be defeated or be slaves to old hurts and habits. We can make choices today. If we choose to be happy and cheerful, we can be.

Right now we can choose to be free of resentment by forgiving old grudges. We can choose to relate rather than isolate. We can be caring, not indifferent. Testiness can be eliminated and replaced with patience. Courage can overcome fear. Anger and irritation can be controlled by tolerance. Frustration can be minimized by acceptance.

We would think it ridiculous if we were asked to choose between happiness and unhappiness, but the sad (and honest) truth is that many of us do choose to be unhappy. What a waste! Blessed are those of us who choose to make the best of things— to make lemonade with the lemons that come our way. All it takes is the desire and the effort. Both come from within. The choice is ours.

Involvement

*By the act of involvement, each individual
begins the lifelong process of paying his
own dues, being a member in good
standing of the society that sustains him.*

Dean John Usher Monroe
Harvard University

Being involved with life means not withdrawing,
not losing our interest in what goes on around
us. As long as we are on Earth, we are part of the
stream of life. If we choose to retreat and disengage,
we not only fail other people, but also put ourselves
in peril.

By never failing to relate to others, by actively
maintaining our interest in local and world affairs,
by keeping abreast of the ongoing hopes, successes,
failures, dreams, struggles, and strivings of our family
members and friends, we stay involved. If the day
comes when we can no longer get around outside our
homes, involvement need not cease. Maybe it will
become necessary to draw in a bit, but will we
become separated from the stream of life? Never!

We make a mistake if we think we have nothing to offer. Lord Byron once said, "To my extreme mortification, I grow wiser every day." We all have a wealth of knowledge, experience, and wisdom to offer our fellow men. Be generous!

Laughing for Our Own Well-Being

The most thoroughly wasted day of all is that on which we have not laughed.
Sebastian Roch Nicolas Chamfort

Experience and common sense tell us that laughter has great physical and psychological benefits. Now scientists are saying so, too. They say that, like exercise, laughter reduces tension. So why not laugh more and feel better?

We may have to retrain ourselves to look on the bright side. One way to do that is to keep a notebook of jokes we read or hear and the laughable happenings we witness. If we stay on the alert, we can usually find at least one funny story a day to write down. Such a notebook becomes a treasure as it gradually fills up.

Norman Cousins, the editor and essayist, used laughter to help himself recover from a serious illness. Since the doctors didn't hold out much hope, Mr. Cousins wrote himself a "humor prescription" and literally "laughed himself well" watching Laurel and Hardy movies and reading funny stories. Because he was wise enough to realize that life is much too important to be taken seriously, he is alive and well today.

It seems that we don't stop laughing because we're old, but we grow old because we stop laughing.

Worry

*Worry never robs tomorrow of its
sorrow; It only saps today of its strength.*
A. J. Cronin

There is a world of difference between worry and concern.

Concern for ourselves and for others is a given for all rational, caring men and women. Everyone we relate to is of concern to us.

Worry is something entirely different. Worry is a state of mind based on fear. If we think we can't help worrying, we must remind ourselves that worry can't help us, either. And besides, as Mark Twain said when he was an old man and had known many troubles, he found that most of the things he worried about never happened. Think of worry as the interest paid by those of us who borrow trouble.

If we are to be healthy mentally, we must not indulge in worry. Arthur Roche described worry graphically: "Worry is a thin stream of fear trickling through the mind. If encouraged, it cuts a channel into which all other thoughts are drained."

Worry *can* be avoided. Remember: the *one* thing each of us has absolute control over is our mind. We are not in charge of the universe, only ourselves.

Being Patronized

*To be nobody but yourself in a world that
seems to be trying to push you into
anonymity means to fight one of the
hardest battles of your life. Never stop
fighting.*

e. e. cummings

Pa-tron-ize: to treat condescendingly. *Con-de-
scend*: to assume an air of superiority. So says
the dictionary.

We were patronized as small children by aggravating relatives. As adults we have all encountered
overbearing officials, doctors, lawyers, or professors.
But somehow, being patronized is more galling now,
in our retirement years.

A long-time actress, complaining about the
prevalent notion that to get acting parts one must be
young, related an experience she had recently. She
went to an interview. The producer, seated at his
desk, was so young he seemed more like a boy. He
did not rise when she entered, but quickly asked,
"What have you done?" In a fury, she replied, "You
first," and walked out of the room. Three cheers for
her! She wins a Golden Chutzpah Award!

Another Golden Chutzpah Award goes to the elderly gentleman whose doctor asked him: "Well, old fella, how far can you see?"

The reply: "I can see the moon and the stars. How far is that?"

What we must try to do is hold our irritation to a minimum and charitably assume that these insensitive people have good intentions. But when the offending individuals are just too much to bear, then politely but firmly let them know we consider their behavior a close encounter of the worst kind. Then we will be worthy of the Golden Chutzpah Award!

Faith in a Higher Power

*Believing is not seeing. I walk in the
shadows of faith. Each step makes me
more certain, toward horizons that are
ever more shrouded in mist.*

Teilhard de Chardin

Ah, the leap in faith it takes to witness so much
tragedy in the world and still believe in a
personal, loving Creator! But how necessary faith is
to a serene life!

For some of us, believing in a caring Higher
Power was never a struggle. But for the rest of us,
the longing to find that Power beyond ourselves has
been a lifelong search. In the springtime of our lives,
many of us were too busy and too self-confident to
think much about such things. Our earthly years
seemed endless then. But, alas, the inevitable disappointments and defeats came along. Events beyond
our control may have driven us to our knees as we
experienced our own limitations and a deep yearning
for something more.

Now, in the winter of our lives, we realize that
our time, like our money, can no longer be spent
extravagantly. Realism tells us that we are mortal and

the issue of faith becomes very real. The will to believe is a spark that must be fanned very carefully now. After all these years, it must not be allowed to die. Many say, "I'll believe it when I see it." Perhaps the truth is, "I'll see it when I believe it." We must never stop hoping and believing and praying. Hold fast! Who is to say that our wavering but living faith may not be the greatest faith of all?

A Memo to Doctors: Old Isn't Senile

Don't accept the unacceptable.
Hugh Prather

*A*geism is a fairly new word in our language. It means a system of false, destructive beliefs about the elderly. It is pervasive in our country, including in the medical profession.

Some research was done recently to determine if doctors treated their elderly patients differently from their younger ones.* The physicians were rated on giving information, questioning, and support. They were also evaluated on whether they were engaged or diffident, patient or impatient, accepting or condescending, respectful or disrespectful. The results of the research showed that the physicians' behavior toward their elderly patients was quite different. They were more patient, engaged, and respectful with their younger patients. Elderly patients were much less successful in getting their doctors to answer their questions and to address their personal concerns. Of course, this isn't true of all doctors. Many of us count our doctor as one of our best friends.

But the results of this report certainly indicate that ageism is pervasive in our country, and often found in the medical profession. What to do? Fight back. While maintaining civility, we must be assertive, insisting that our questions be answered and that we be treated with respect.

*This report appeared in *Language and Communication* (vol. 6, pp. 113-24).

Reaching Out

The tragedy of life is not what men suffer,
but what they miss.

Thomas Carlyle

The Bible instructs us to bear one another's burdens. And many of us have done so in the past,
when our resources were greater and we felt more
powerful. Now we may feel that such responsibility
belongs to younger people. Our own burdens seem
overwhelming sometimes—how could we possibly
take on more?

But there is a paradox here: helping others often
does as much for us as it does for the people we're
helping. Responding to another person's trouble
rewards us with balance and perspective. It's impossible to reach out a helping hand without deepening
awareness that we aren't the only ones who are hurting.
And sharing someone else's struggle also means that we
can share their successes, no matter how small those
victories may be. As they gain heart, we do, too. As
we express concern, we have less opportunity or need
to express narrow self-centeredness.

We have all seen, in photographs or real life,
farmers carrying buckets, one on each end of a pole,

across their shoulders. For us, carrying just one bucket in that fashion would be extremely difficult—maybe impossible. For us, too, it is really easier to share a friend's load along with our own than to go it alone.

Play

Man's most serious activity is play.
George Santayana

A life without some play is incomplete, and, more than that, it is actually unhealthy. It is tragic if we have no merriment or fun, no enjoyment in our lives.

Having fun has myriad facets. There is the fun of watching humorous movies and plays, and of reading literature that makes us laugh (or at least chuckle). Fun for many is playing games—bridge, canasta, Scrabble, Jeopardy, or whatever. Others of us play golf, swim, or participate in other physical activities. For many of us the ultimate choice, and the most satisfying, is playing with our grandchildren. Children, with their spontaneity and sparkle, help us rekindle our own playfulness and festive spirit. It is also important to seek out positive, happy people for our friends. Simply pausing to enjoy the beauty in the world around us is another form of gentle fun.

Never put off enjoyment, because there's no time like the pleasant. (Please forgive the pun.) Believe in appreciating life. Be sure to have fun every day.

Pain

*I have now joined the fellowship
of those who live in pain.*

Dr. Thomas Dooley

Chronic pain is different from acute pain, which rises rapidly and then subsides (for example, stubbing a toe, biting your cheek). Chronic pain is of long duration and sometimes extreme severity. Certainly, it is not limited to the elderly, but incidences increase with age, and it is destructive.

For those of us who have joined the fellowship of those who live in pain, it is imperative that we fight off despair and depression. While it is true we have pain, pain will not have us. We know that overuse of drugs may lead to addiction. There are other approaches, other possibilities, to investigate. One approach is involvement in a good pain control program that includes relaxation techniques, imagery, and self-hypnosis. Then, too, there are national chronic pain outreach associations that sponsor local self-help chapters. Also, many hospitals have pain clinics.

The absolute must in living day in and day out with pain and discomfort is to become involved in projects that are of interest, and then *willing* the mind to cease focusing on the pain.

If "courage" is grace under pressure, as Hemingway said, then with grace we must and will persevere. We are stronger than we think.

Biological Aging

Know thyself.
Inscription on the temple of Apollo at Delphi

The life processes for all living beings are well understood today. It is estimated that the relatively fixed longevity for humans is between 110 and 120 years.

There are several theories of the biological basis of aging. It is not clear whether the differences in longevity among us are inherited or due to freedom from disease. Recently, "longevity genes" have been identified that cause the production of low levels of a necessary cell material. These become more prevalent in those in their eighties and nineties. Another theory, known as the program theory, maintains that longevity and aging are predetermined at the gene level in the same way as growth and development are. Another theory states that aging results from the cumulative damage to cellular DNA. It has also been suggested that a genetically determined appearance of certain proteins that cause cell death occurs. It is widely known that the total number of neurons progressively declines with age.

The change in cells, tissues, organs, and organ

systems is inevitable. But our lifestyles can cause these changes to occur more slowly and at a later date. Healthful living is the key. A tenet of modern medical science is that the reserve in all organ systems is sufficient to maintain a stable balance (homeostasis) well into the tenth decade for most individuals. So, knowing ourselves means recognizing the realities of aging while at the same time knowing how to take good care of ourselves.

Listening

To listen is to receive.
Elie Wiesel

One of the primary requisites of a good counselor is to know how to listen—really listen. It is a skill we should all practice. And, like all efforts we make for others, the benefits spill over on us in one way or another.

We should listen to others even if what they say turns us off. We never know when we will be enlightened and made wiser, even by people we don't agree with. Listen to a friend who feels the need to express his or her depression or despair. Recognize how he or she is feeling and encourage more discussion. Express your understanding and empathy.

Above all, it is necessary to listen, wholeheartedly, with our *full* attention—eyes, ears, emotions, and hearts. There is communication other than verbal. The eyes, facial expression, and even posture speak loud and clear to those who truly listen. We have all, at one time or another, had the annoying experience of trying to talk with someone we knew was not really listening to what we were saying.

Listening is probably the most important communication skill of all, and it can be learned. Try to hear people's feelings—listen for what they are saying, as well as what they are not saying, and try to understand what they mean. You will not hear if you don't listen.

The Loss of a Friend

*So life goes on. For years we plant the
seed, we feel ourselves rich, and then
come the years when time does its work
and our plantation is made sparse and
thin. One by one, our comrades slip
away, depriving us of their shade.*

Antoine de Saint-Exupery

What shock and sadness engulf us when we hear of the death of a friend, especially when the news is unexpected! Now there is another empty niche somewhere in our hearts.

One of the inscriptions in the antechamber of King Tut's tomb reads: "To speak of the dead is to cause them to live again." We may well add that fond memories of our friends will cause them to live again. So, although we mustn't repress our feelings of sadness, we must not dwell morbidly on the past, but concentrate with gratitude on our good fortune to have had such splendid friends for so many years.

And so we continue to go forward, open to the future but fortified by memories of dear friends who have weighed anchor and sailed away.

Children

*I have a kind of hunger for the sturdy,
independent little bodies of children, the
boundless energy, the wonderful,
uncompromising self-confidence.*

Abigail Lewis

Most of us were blessed with children when we were younger and now enjoy our grand-children, and even our great-grandchildren, if we are fortunate. (How quickly the years slip by!) For those of us who did not raise a family, probably there are nieces and nephews and children of friends whom we have enjoyed through the years.

In a tribute to his daughter, Will Durant writes: "It is enough for us that she has come, and that into this life so questionable in origin and so obscure in destiny, her laughter and her guilelessness have brought sparkling fountains of delight." Sometimes, while our children were growing up, they tried us— oh, how they tried us! But the positive far outweighed the negative. The icing on the cake was the arrival of grandchildren. What a thrill and a privilege it is to contribute to their lives, as well as to the lives of our children.

It is a thrill and a privilege, and also a welcome responsibility. The lasting legacy we can leave our children and their children is pride in who they are and where they came from, which will be the incentive to achieve a fulfilled and productive life.

Dying

No death can shield me in a shroud . . . I
go to brother with the grass and with the
sunning leave . . . O little house that
sheltered me, Dissolve again in wind and
rain, to be Part of the cosmic weird
Economy. . . .

John Neihardt

It is imperative for our own peace of mind that we
realistically accept that we are mortals. Death
belongs to life, as birth does. We should try to
acknowledge and then resolve all apprehension and
fear we have of death. No doubt, this must ultimately
be the most difficult task that human beings face.
Because of our gift of intelligence and reflection, we
alone know that we are finite. Once the inevitability
of our own death has been accepted bravely and with
equanimity, then we are able to proceed with the rest
of the time that has been allotted to us with maximum
energy and happiness, knowing that our Higher
Power is *love*.

Dylan Thomas advised his father, "Do not go
gentle into that good night, / Old age should burn
and rave at close of day; / Rage, rage against the

dying of the light." Perhaps the far better way to face our own death is expressed by Annie Dillard: "I think that the dying pray at last not 'please,' but 'thank you,' as a guest thanks his host at the door. . . . And then you walk fearlessly. . . . I go my way, and my left foot says 'Glory' and my right foot says 'Amen.' "

Adversity

*Even the severed branch grows again, and
the sunken moon returns. Wise men who
ponder this are not troubled in adversity.*
Indian proverb

It is a good idea, when we seem to be getting the
very worst of things, to make the best of it. Think
of the teakettle. When it is up to its neck in hot
water, it whistles!

Most of us have faced adversity; many of us
have experienced bitter, heartbreaking adversity.
Remember what philosopher Nietzsche tells us: "That
which does not kill me makes me stronger." While
we may often feel that maybe we would settle for
not being made so strong if we could avoid adversity,
unfortunately, it is not a matter of choice. Since it
cannot be avoided, the wise thing is to make our
misfortunes work for us—to derive some good from
our hard times.

When we get to the end of our rope, we must
tie a knot and hang on. If we can believe that every
adversity brings with it the seeds of an equivalent
advantage, this conviction can help to sustain us in
dark and desperate hours.

Living Alone

*What life means to us is determined not so
much by what life brings as by the
attitude we bring to life; not so much by
what happens to us as by our reaction to
what happens.*

Lewis Dunning

A Ziggy cartoon shows Ziggy sneezing and sneezing and sneezing. Then he says, "God bless me!"
The final caption reads, ". . .the first warning sign of
livingaloneness." Well, God bless Ziggy! If there is no
one else around to do it, why not give yourself a
blessing?

It is a given that living alone is far better than
living in an unpleasant situation with other people.
But it is also true that living alone is second best to a
loving, shared household. However, second best is
not so bad, unless we make it so.

Think of some advantages. We are free to come
and go at our own pleasure; listen to the kind of
music that pleases us; eat where, what, and when we
choose; watch what we want on television (with the
blessed privilege of turning it off if we choose). Other
advantages will come to mind with a little reflection.

These may be small advantages compared to *the real thing*, but nevertheless, they *are* advantages. Thinking along these lines will prevent the slow poison of self-pity from engulfing those of us who now live alone.

Pacing Ourselves

The race is not always to the swift, but to those who keep running.

Poster

After years and years of frenzied activity, often with barely enough time to sleep, it should be no surprise that, finally, our energy is not what it used to be. We begin to feel our vitality ebb a bit.

Now is the time to recognize and accept that we can no longer keep up all the activities previously considered so essential. It is time to reconsider and say no when we become aware of our current limitations. Think of us as candles no longer blazing furiously in the wind, but with our flames still steadily burning on.

It is a time to pace ourselves. It is a time to be honest with ourselves and seek a balance. There is no need, and no reason, to, as Henry Wadsworth Longfellow says, "fold our tents" and withdraw completely. On the other hand, it is foolhardy to risk exhaustion because we cannot come to terms with the fact that our capacity and energy have diminished. It is not necessary to be in the fast lane in order to be happy. There is much pleasure left even if we are now running at the back of the pack.

Since we don't know whether we have one mile to go or a hundred "before we sleep," as Robert Frost puts it, it is only wise and prudent to no longer burn the candle at both ends.

Health

*People in good physical shape not only
tend to live longer, look better, and have
more energy, they also tend to have fewer
emotional problems.*
      Arkansas Rehabilitation Center bulletin

It is no secret that the blessing of good health
depends on several factors, some of which we
contribute to and some of which are beyond our
control. The longevity of our parents, certainly a
matter of chance, is one of the most important
elements. Environmental factors such as poor air
quality and noise pollution adversely affect our
health.

However, we contribute to our own decline with
poor health habits. The good thing about this is that
we can do something about it if we really want to.
It's not too late to change old habits for new and
better ones. Where there is a will, there is a way—
even to start a simple, safe exercise program. It
doesn't need to cost one cent, or be overly unpleasant. Try exercising on a regular basis while standing
in front of the television set watching the morning
news before breakfast. It must be consistent! Discuss

your proper weight with your doctor. Today, information on proper diet is everywhere. Of course, we are all quite aware of the devastating effects of tobacco and alcohol.

That good health slows the process of aging has been known for a very long time. Good health gives us great endurance, relieves tension, and grants us energy and vigor. What could be more worthwhile?

Grief

*And, ultimately, the fact must be faced
that grief is never fully resolved, that the
hole in life is never filled up again, and
that there is a permanent pain of
loneliness, which is remembrance's somber
and valuable witness to life.*

Bernadine Kreis and Alice Pattie
Up from Grief

All of us who have experienced the loss of our significant other, our lifelong partner, have learned that there remains a permanent pain—a particular place of emptiness in our hearts that will never be filled.

Nor would we want it erased. The beautiful words of Tennyson reveal our sorrow and distress: "But / Oh for the touch of a vanished hand, / And the sound of a voice that is still!" However, while our loss is crushing, those of us blessed with faith in a loving God can rejoice in the knowledge that our loved one is safe and happier far beyond our understanding. So take solace!

And so life goes on. Never quite the same. Never as *complete* as it once was.

But we still have our memories which nothing will destroy. They are our treasure. And those memories can be ingots of gold as we continue on our journey!

Action

Whatever you can do, or think you can,
begin it. Boldness has genius, power,
and magic.

Goethe

To live is to take risks and to be involved. Sometimes when we are in chronic pain or threatened with despair, the idea of withdrawing—ceasing to make an effort—is terribly inviting.

We must resist, though, if at all possible, because that is the road to deep depression. The first step to awareness and action is the struggle with oneself. It becomes our battle to *be*. We are all so individualized that forms of actions to be pursued are varied. If we feel that the walls are beginning to close in, it is time to open up, stretch out, and refuse to be overwhelmed by the "slings and arrows of outrageous fortune."

Some surefire paths of action are learning a new skill, making new friends, trying something new (food, clothes, exercise), offering our expertise on projects. We should let our actions involve us physically, emotionally, and spiritually. David Lloyd George said: "Don't be afraid to take a big step if one is indicated; you can't cross a chasm in two small steps."

Appreciating Others

Appreciation is a wonderful thing; it makes what is excellent in others belong to us as well.

Voltaire

When we contemplate the contributions other people have made to our lives, it is humbling. Think of all the tremendous breakthroughs that have occurred due to others' fertile minds and energies. Also, there are the small benefits we enjoy every day that would be nonexistent if it were not for other people's ingenuity.

Then, too, most of us need to be more aware of kindnesses from not only our most significant others, but also from acquaintances, neighbors, and service people. Good neighbors are treasures. Acquaintances who greet you with a smile and service people who do their best to earn your trust should also be prized.

Albert Einstein, on the subject of appreciation, said it well: "A hundred times every day I remind myself that my inner and outer life depends on the labor of other men, living and dead, and that I must exert myself in order to give in the same measure that I have received and am still receiving."

Solitude

*Language has created the word
"loneliness" to express the pain of being
alone, and the word "solitude" to express
the glory of being alone.*

Paul Tillich

Solitude and loneliness are not synonyms. Being alone can be a markedly different experience from being lonely. It is quite possible (and often happens) that we are lonely while surrounded by other people. Loneliness doesn't mean without people. It means something else. It means depressingly lonely.

Solitude can, and should, be experienced in a positive way. When the benefits of solitude are realized, we are able to enjoy new insights into our lives. Solitude offers us a retreat, a shelter—asylum from the absurdities that threaten us. Solitude can be like the eye of a hurricane—a calm spot surrounded by the screaming winds of life with all its problems. All the great spiritual leaders knew the necessity for solitude. They sought refuge again and again in quiet places where they could be restored.

Few of us can go to the desert to find solitude, but we can all find it someplace, if we wish to. In order to have the optimum life as we grow older, we must seek solitude (not loneliness) to grow inwardly closer to God as we know Him, and find tranquility of spirit.

Determination

Dear God, the plans I tried to carry
through have failed. I will not sorrow.
I'll pause a little while, Dear God,
and try again tomorrow.

John Fico

More often than not these days, as we grow older, the path we wish to travel seems more difficult and arduous. If we ever needed determination, now is the time.

Determination to hold on to our achievements and our abilities must be the motivator now. It takes determination to keep going when our bodies hurt and our spirits begin to flag. But it pays off beyond measure. If we lack determination to persevere, whether it be with a good health regimen, with prayer, with meaningful relationships, or whatever, we will meet with disaster. It is giving up on life, and none of us wants to travel that road.

Everything worthwhile takes determination and effort. There is no way we can run away from the problems we are faced with at this stage of our lives.

Everything worthwhile takes determined effort. It takes a little longer to get to the door when we hear opportunity knocking, but if we are determined, we'll get there!

Enthusiasm

So long as enthusiasm lasts, so long is youth still with us.

David Jordan

It could be that an enthusiastic attitude and an optimistic frame of mind are the most vital weapons we have against decline and deterioration. Every facet of our lives requires enthusiasm if we are to "fight the good fight" (1 Tim. 6:12).

Vince Lombardi, the great football coach, used to tell his team that if they were not fired with enthusiasm, they would be fired from the team with enthusiasm. We are not threatened with being fired from a job in these years of retirement, but anyone lacking enthusiasm in his or her daily pursuits is threatened with stagnation and discontent. Like any other good habit, enthusiasm is strengthened with practice. And when we show enthusiasm, it uplifts others as well as ourselves. Enthusiasm really is contagious, and so is the lack of it. Think of times in your life when you were all fired up about something, and then were shot down by the disinterest and indifference of others. But the opposite has also happened. A truly enthusiastic person is hard to resist, and tends to fire us up.

The bottom line is that we can choose to be enthusiastic, and practice to make it so. We need to *live*, not just exist, all the days of our lives!

Friendship

*Who would be happy, first must have
a friend.*

Edgar Guest

Can you imagine what life would be like without friendship? How lonely, flat, and burdensome! How many times have we said to a friend, "I couldn't have made it without you!"

Friends come in all shapes and sizes, some more involved in our lives than others. Many are old friends we have known almost longer than we can remember. The devastation we feel when an old friend leaves us is proof of the importance of friendship. There is no ulterior motive in true friendship, only the deepening of our spirits. Therein lies the refreshment. And what a consolation and solace it is to be able to pour out our frustrations and disappointments to a caring and understanding friend. Pancho Villa once said, "The man I call brother is the one who guards my back." It is calming to know that our friends will "guard our backs." Of course, we must share our best (not just worst) times with our friends, also. If they endure the ebb of our tide, they should get to share the flood, as well. Sharing laughter and the good times with friends doubles the pleasure.

Ralph Waldo Emerson said it wisely: "A friend may well be reckoned the masterpiece of nature."

Giving and Receiving

Blessed are those who can give without remembering and receive without forgetting.

Elizabeth Bibesco

Life is such a give-and-take. Mark Twain once said that the best way to cheer yourself up was to try to cheer up someone else.

Money isn't all there is to give. It is when we give of ourselves that we truly give. We give love, we give respect, we give our attention, we give our encouragement, we give our time—the list is endless. And the more we give, the more we receive, in so many different ways.

There are also the times when we are needy. Others offer us sustenance and assistance, and we humbly accept. Our gratitude, which we hope we always express, can only truly be repaid in kind somewhere else down the line. If we are generous in our giving and appreciative in our receiving, we have mastered the art of living the good life. All of us have experienced the truth of this.

Appreciation Owed to God

How can we thank God enough?
1 Thess. 3:9

The movie *The Color Purple* expresses so vividly the central theme of the appreciation we owe to God for all our blessings, including the blessing of a field of purple flowers. Our blessings are myriad, and yet how callous and insensitive we become!

How God puts up with our ingratitude is difficult to understand. Everyone can benefit from consciously concentrating on God's gifts to us. Saying grace before meals, somewhat out of style these days, can be a simple act of gratitude (said in silence, if we wish) and takes so little time and effort. Grace said before a meal can consist of a short sentence, such as "Bless us, O Lord, and this food from your bounty." Prayers of petition come easily, but we should never forget prayers of thanksgiving.

Appreciation is due to God for all the beauty of our world—the precious smile of a baby, the gorgeous sunrise and sunset, all the loveliness of nature, the warmth of friends and loved ones, our complicated and superbly functioning bodies, and our Godlike minds. There is no way we can thank Him *adequately, but if we stop trying and become indifferent, we are the losers. Then we are diminished.

Keeping Your Mind Fit

*The best cosmetic in the world is an
active mind that is always finding
something new.*

                              Mary M. Atkinson

Surely one of the worst hazards confronting us is
the tendency to close our minds to the fresh and
new around us. First, consider all the ideas, innova-
tions, and inventions that have been around for many,
many years but can be rediscovered by us if we look
for them. Then, consider all the truly new ways of
doing things—the seemingly miraculous tools in science
and medicine that seem to appear each day.

Keeping abreast of the new vocabulary evolving
along with all these new things is no small task.
Twenty years ago, words such as microchip, quark,
videodisc, and gene-splicing did not exist. A 1947
dictionary defines spaceship as a "projected" plane for
interplanetary travel, and DNA and CAT scan are
nowhere to be found. There are many opportunities
open to us to keep current and to be interested (and
interesting). In addition to reading and watching
informative television, we have excellent enrichment
courses available to us. Most universities and junior

colleges offer noncredit courses for continuing education for those with active minds that are always looking for something new.

William James once said that often people think they are thinking when all they are doing is rearranging their prejudices. Today, more and more of us are *thinking*, and thereby escaping old prejudices. It takes openness to grow.

Loneliness

*To know loneliness means
to experience life.*

Clark Moustakas

Do you remember when you first experienced loneliness? Chances are you were quite young—maybe as young as four or five. It might have been when your parents left for a weekend, or when your very best friend moved away, or when you were sent to your room for some naughtiness. Yes, loneliness has been a part of our lives on occasion for a long time.

Now, as we grow older, loneliness is ever more familiar. Our "forest of friends grows thinner," and after retirement our contacts diminish. There are two ways to combat loneliness: by reaching out and by reaching within. Both are required if we are to defeat loneliness, and they are of equal importance. We are lonely because we build walls instead of bridges. Being honestly interested in others will defeat loneliness every time. Numerous are the means of mingling, and they are available to us—through our church affiliation, volunteering, offering our neighbor friendship, participation in activities at senior citizen centers, etc. But no matter how successfully we fill up our lives with family and friends, there will always be the alone times—they are a necessity if we are to have balance. We must not let the alone times be filled with self-pity or despair or fear; instead, let them be times of enrichment, nourishment, and thanksgiving.

We need to recognize loneliness for what it is— an unpleasant human condition that can be faced and overcome.

Memories

*God gave us memories so we might have
roses in December.*

Poster

Happy memories never pass. We can go back into
our yesterdays *once in awhile*, and treat our
minds to dear and lovely memories. It is a source of
escape *for a short time* from the present—from
sometimes unpleasant realities.

The key, of course, is "for a short time." Like
everything else in life, a balance is required. There is
a danger of living in the past, which does happen to
some older people. It is dangerous to stay in a frozen
sea of memories. We must be in the ongoing, rushing
current of life. With that warning in mind, we are
free to indulge ourselves for a time, now and then, in
recalling some of the happenings of years gone by. It
has been said that memories are a nursery where old
children play with broken toys. Maybe so, but we
know that occasional play is good for us.

Neihardt said it best in *Twilight of the Sioux*.
An old Indian, reminiscing by the campfire, says:

"What matter? It was good!
Why mourn the young flame laughing in the wood
With tears upon the ashes? I could laugh
All night remembering, forgetting half
The happy times before the world was old.
Do you remember, friends?"

Not Giving Up

*The greatest loss in life is what dies inside
us while we live.*

Norman Cousins

Giving up is the ultimate tragedy that must be avoided at all costs. Tomorrow things may change for the better. Why not? Everything is possible. Never use the word *never*.

One of the most common causes of failure and giving in to despair is quitting or giving up when we are overtaken by temporary setbacks. We only fail when we stop trying. Our instinct to preserve a vital life force within runs deep—we must draw on it in moments of dejection and discouragement. Let's resolve today to be unafraid, to approach our problems with an intrepid and determined spirit.

At the very least we can be like the man who said, "I guess I didn't win, but I didn't lose, either. I'm just going to come out even." The only way we are going to lose is by giving up.

Baba Hari Dass said, "You must save yourself. It is your duty."

Putting Ourselves Down

You are a child of the Universe . . . you have a right to be here.

Desiderata

We are really going to make our lives miserable if we put ourselves down. It is so distressing to hear someone say, "I was *only* a mechanic," "I was *only* a secretary," or "I am *only* a burden," "I am *only* a housewife," or "I am *only* a grandparent." Such nonsense! Not only must we not say such things, we must not even *think* along those lines.

We must be proud of our lives now, as well as what we have accomplished in the past. We are annoyed when others patronize us, and yet we tend to turn around and inflict the very same kind of behavior upon ourselves. The measure of our worth in our youth and now has nothing to do with money, prestige, or fame, but is based on our integrity, wholeness, and sincerity.

We need to be thinking in this fashion: "The young people today are getting so smart they could almost be our age." And mean it! We have every right to be proud of ourselves—who we are and where we are. If we don't think well of ourselves, how can we expect others to have a high opinion of us?

Overcoming Obstacles to Happiness

There are two ways to meet difficulties: you can alter the difficulty or you can alter yourself.

Phyllis Bottome

Certainly there is no shortage of obstacles to our happiness these days. Of course, we have been confronted with obstacles of all kinds throughout our lifetime. Maybe it just *seems* like there are more now. No matter—they are here and they are real.

Most of us, sooner or later, will be faced with problems related to housing, transportation, health care, relationships, and many other parts of our lives. The obstacles are going to be twice as difficult if we attempt to deal with them by ourselves. There is a great deal of help available to us these days—group travel, seminars, clinics, lifetime learning programs, exercise classes, and Meals on Wheels for the housebound. Of course, we also need to be aware of and take an honest look at our attitude toward some of our difficulties. Maybe we need to make some changes in ourselves—be less demanding, more accepting, less contrary, more pleasant—in order to combat obstacles to happiness.

A successful life should be measured not by how much wealth has been accumulated, but rather by the obstacles overcome. We are doing very well if we just keep trying as best we can to keep a healthy distance between us and all things mean and hurtful.

Quitting

A quitter never wins, and a winner never quits.

Proverb

Quitting is not for us. Our life experience is too positive, our investment too vital, our contribution too worthwhile to let it all end in defeat. Now, the time when we may be most tempted to quit, is the time our measure is truly taken.

Throwing in the towel is easy. Whether quitting is in the form of apathy, withdrawal, or, Heaven forbid, suicide, it is a shameful way of throwing God's gift to us in His face. Life doesn't have to come to such a sorry state (and it seldom does) if we don't try to live it alone. Everyone needs to reach out to his Higher Power and to friends when the going gets rough. If we find someone with whom to talk things over, or let it all out in prayer, help will come. Trouble not shared is doubled and can lead to disaster.

When it seems we are in the last ditch, we mustn't quit. Before any of us start thinking of traveling down the slippery road of quitting, we must turn back and avoid the harsh face of futility and despair. We must determine not to give up, but be "heroes in the strife." A life lived bravely to the end lights the way for others. This is no small thing.

Regrets

Never let yesterday use up today.
Proverb

Since it seems we only go around once and that there is no turning back, why waste precious time on such futility as bemoaning the irreversible? All of us have done things or said things, both minor and major, that we regret. But if we are to live happy, fulfilled lives, these must be relegated to time gone by and not be allowed to poison our present lives.

Our sole goal now must be oriented toward the future, whether it be tomorrow, next week, or next year. We really don't have time to waste mulling over past mistakes. It is so useless. The only thing regrets are good for is to steer us away from past mistakes.

It is self-destructive to feel guilty about the past. What's done is done. As long as we have learned from any mistakes we might have made, there need be no lingering self-incrimination.

Smiling

They might not need me–yet they might–
I'll let my Heart be just in sight–
A smile so small as mine might be
Precisely their necessity.

Emily Dickinson

There are facial smiles and there are vocal smiles, too. Both contribute to and enhance our existence. Just for a minute, imagine living one day without any smiles given or received—how blah, flat, and gloomy.

It has been said that a smile is a curve that helps to set things straight. And, it's free. How many things are free these days? Precious few. It only takes a minimum of effort to give one and costs nothing to receive. There is a bonus involved with smiling: the smile we send out returns to us, if only in a warm, uplifting feeling. Here is another benefit to be considered: a smile takes only seventeen muscles, a frown takes forty-three! Smile wrinkles are so much more attractive than frown ones.

Here is what Joseph Addison had to say about

smiles long ago:

"What sunshine is to flowers, smiles are to humanity.

They are but trifles, but scattered along life's Pathway the good they do is inconceivable.

Smiles still are 'humanity's sunshine' three hundred years later, and they always will be. Create a little sunshine with a smile—the whole world will be better for it."

Understanding

More light.
Goethe's last words

We have some understanding of the world around us and of the people around us. We will never understand everything; some things will just never make sense to us. But understanding our fellow man should be an ongoing occupation of ours.

Understanding people seems to lead to compassion. That is to say, true understanding of another's problems and pain can only result in compassionate empathy. It is not necessary to have experienced the identical hurt in order to understand, but only to have known pain and failure of whatever kind ourselves. We all fit that requirement.

Much hatred and hostility could be eliminated, to the enormous benefit of the hated, as well as the hater, if an attempt to understand were initiated. Understanding, to whatever degree we are able, requires an open mind and a nonjudgmental attitude on our part. It calls for a generous spirit. We all have known "holier-than-thou" people who refuse to make even the smallest effort to understand a different point of view. They are crippled. The more we try to understand others, to "walk in their shoes," the more compassionate we become.

In a manner of speaking, we can be caterpillars that have found their butterfly wings. And while understanding doesn't necessarily mean condoning, it does mean finding openness, empathy, and awareness.

Work

*It is well with me only when I have a
chisel in my hand.*

Michelangelo

The dictionary defines *work* as "toil, labor," but
also as "achievement, effort." In these materialistic times we associate work with making money. But
we know, upon reflection, that there can be deeper
satisfactions and greater rewards than money. In the
quotation above, Michelangelo didn't say, "It is well
with me only when I am being well paid for having
a chisel in my hand."

More power to those of us still in the work
force. The recent legislation outlawing age discrimination and compulsory retirement was long overdue.
However, the majority of us are no longer fighting
the early morning traffic, the lunch crunch, the daily
grind. This doesn't mean we are idle. Far from it.
This is the time when we have the opportunity to do
our best work, because we are doing what we want
to do. For example, the retired salesman can now
teach a class in salesmanship at the local community
school; the activists can make a difference in so many
areas (environmental, racial discrimination, child

abuse); and those involved in neighborhood improvement associations and all manner of volunteer activities can help their communities. Then there are all the different kinds of work we do strictly for our own pleasure, such as gardening, needlework, woodworking, all sorts of repair work, even writing.

Isn't it true that the best prize life has to offer is the chance to work with enthusiasm at something that is worth doing?

Our Attitudes toward Aging

Age is just experience; some of us are
more experienced than others.

                              Mickey Rooney

Consider our attitude on aging—not the attitude of younger people toward us, but our own. A few of us become fixated on the disappointments, but most of us, like Mickey Rooney, choose to emphasize the positive aspects.

We would be less than honest if we refused to admit that there are some aspects of aging that are the pits. But we still can be the best we have ever been in many areas—wisdom, compassion, know-how, and judgment are just a few. All things considered, growing old is not so bad unless we allow our attitude toward life to sour. If we don't place value on our own lives, why be surprised if others don't value us? Respect breeds respect. It is all a matter of attitude.

If it is true, as the Talmud says, that we do not see things as they are, but as we are, then the beauty of life is that we alone control our thoughts, our attitudes. No one but us can change our own attitudes. If we choose to, we can think of ourselves not as old, but as just more experienced!

Bravery

The hero is no braver than the ordinary
man, but he is brave five minutes longer.
                                    Ralph Waldo Emerson

To live our lives any way other than bravely is an act of absurdity. Shakespeare wrote, "Cowards die many times before their deaths; / The valiant never taste of death but once."

Most of us have never had our bravery tested in dramatic ways like the war hero, or the person who rescued someone from a burning building, or the father who swam between his daughter and a shark, or the many others who have risked their lives to save others. But all of us have been called on to act bravely countless times in our lives. There have been times when we persevered when we so very much wanted to quit, when we thought we couldn't go on but did anyway, when we continued to make an effort even though we were sure we didn't have a chance, when we felt we would surely be vanquished and yet did not surrender. Like Daniel, the lions didn't eat us because we were mostly grit and the rest of us was backbone. Or maybe our bravery was really that we were the only ones who knew we were afraid.

Now is the time, as much as ever (maybe even more), to live bravely, banishing fear and panic. When it gets dark enough, the brave spirit sees the stars.

Sexuality

There is nothing ridiculous in love.
Olive Schreiner

It is commonly believed that older adults don't need sex, don't want it, and can't do it. The truth is that sexuality is lifelong.

There is no physical reason for sexual appetite to diminish. The primary problem is a wrong attitude that society encourages. Often that is used as an excuse to avoid sex. Sometimes adult children resent their parent's dating, feeling it is unseemly and in bad taste. That attitude is probably not as prevailing as it used to be. Another myth on its way out is to think of an older adult still interested in sex as a "dirty old man" or "dirty old woman."

Financial losses involved in remarriage have been a real problem to many who have been fortunate enough to find another to share their lives. Happily, the Social Security laws have been amended to erase this obstacle almost completely. Modern medicine has made great strides in helping women with hysterectomies and menopausal problems by prescribing estrogen therapy.

Those of us who feel uneasy about our sexuality should discuss it with trusted friends, pastors, physicians, or counselors. Sexuality is a part of life—forever!

Retirement

Retirement syndrome blues can be fatal if you allow them to be.

Albert Rosenfeld

Retirement syndrome blues are real. They afflict some of us, but not all. It is encouraging to know that such a sad and self-destructive attitude toward retirement is neither typical nor common. But, nevertheless, it does painfully assail some of us. Severe depression, sometimes even resulting in suicide, does indeed occur.

Willy Loman, in *Death of a Salesman*, epitomized the emotional and physical condition known as the "retirement syndrome." He suffered acute anxiety and depression which culminated in his suicide. We know that a positive outlook on life has a positive effect on both physical and emotional well-being, and that also the opposite is true—a rigid refusal to accept retirement adversely affects both mind and body. At age eighty, Ben Franklin advised us that keeping up our spirits would keep up our bodies. It is known that depression (a form of stress) actually affects brain chemistry.

There is a tribe in Australia that believes a man can lose his soul, and when they think that has happened, the man and the tribe attempt to bring about his death by performing funeral services and making it clear that he is to die. While we certainly judge such behavior to be barbaric, there is a correlation, in a way, to our society's forcing still-capable, competent people to retire—stealing their souls, you might say. But how foolish of these people to allow their jobs to become their souls in the first place! No one on his or her deathbed ever said, "I wish I had spent more time at work."

Spirituality

There are two roads in life, the black and the red. The red road is the spiritual road. When on the red road, we can journey through any country in peace.

Lakota Indian teaching

The Lakotas say it well, don't they? They believe we are made with a yearning to walk the spiritual road with our Creator. No running away from or toward anything, but a journey with our God.

There is a bond of love between one person and another, and between people and their Creator, that is what we call spirituality. In our sophisticated and materialistic society, our way along "the red road" is difficult to follow. It is obscured by the noisy turmoil and rush of modern life, and most of that turmoil and rush signifies less than nothing. How we cheat ourselves when we neglect the spiritual side of our being! When we open our hearts, when we seek to become attuned to the spirit of God as we understand Him, our lives become less burdened, more in harmony with our world.

Robert Browning wrote: "Earth's crammed with heaven, And every common bush afire with God;

But only he who sees takes off his shoes."

Time spent developing and nurturing our spirituality is what allows us to be "he who sees and takes off his shoes." God does not need to seem far away. He didn't move. Like everything worthwhile in life, the spiritual path must be a choice. Fortified with this wise choice, we can now "journey through any country in peace."

Today

I have no Yesterdays,
Time took them away;
Tomorrow may not be—
But I have Today.

Pearl McGinnis

Our life experiences of all the past years, so very rich and meaningful to us, are now in our memory banks, available for enjoyable recall at any time. However, our memories were then; this is *now*. We must learn to build all our roads on today because tomorrow's ground is too uncertain.

As far as we know, we only go around once, so our time is truly precious and not to be wasted. As the poem says, "Tomorrow may not be." But today is ours to do with as we will. Life might be thought of as a bank. Each day we withdraw our allotted hours and proceed to spend them either well or wastefully. All days need not show great achievement. If we are exhausted and must rest today to let our cups fill up—that is well. If today is a high-energy day (God be praised!) and much is to be accomplished, that is well, too. Very well, indeed!

The only wasted days are those when we allow self-pity, self-destructive thoughts, envy, giving up, or giving in to get the upper hand. The day has been given to us, a gift for sure, and gifts are not meant to be ignored, disregarded, or left unappreciated. Like all gifts, this day is to be enjoyed, appreciated, and valued.

It is a tragedy to put off living to the fullest. Why dream of some enchanting happening when all about us there is magic every day?

Self-Pity

Perhaps the greatest cause of unhappiness is self-pity.

Dennis Wholey

Self-pity is slow poison. It is counterproductive and self-destructive. No one would question that in this last quarter of our lives we are confronted with all manner of happenings, from the insignificant to the significant, that might warrant self-pity. The list is endless: eyesight dimming, hair thinning, stamina waning, the entire body creaking. Even more traumatic, our number of friends is diminishing. Inevitably, our world narrows.

These things should come as no surprise; all were to be expected. If we are faced with more difficulties now than when we were younger, that is all right, because we are stauncher and more durable, having been weathered by life's storms.

There are even some tradeoffs, if we look for them. Life is calmer, fewer demands are made on us, and we have more free time, fewer obligations, maybe even more choices about some things. There is really no excuse for self-pity if we keep our heads on straight. Wallowing in self-pity is self-defeating. It is beneath us. We must not get caught in that trap.

Patience

Have patience with all things, but first of all with yourself.

Saint Francis de Sales

It has been wisely said that the best course of action is to adapt the pace of nature; her secret is patience. All our stewing, fretting, and agitation results in nothing but mental anguish.

Being patient with ourselves is a matter of attitude and outlook. Patience can become a habit with a little insight and practice. So what if we cannot remember a name, title, or date? That has happened all of our lives; it just happens a little more frequently these days. Generally, if we wait a bit, the answer will come to us. It may take a little longer to get out of bed in the morning, to walk around the block, even to eat a meal. We may wish we had the old hustle, but since we don't, we must be patient with ourselves and accept the new rhythm.

Daily interaction with others requires patience, too. Of course, it always has, but now, perhaps, successful coping requires forbearance more than it ever did. If we are to maintain our mental health and equanimity, we must practice patience and tolerance in all manner of situations—differences with our children, public slights, other people's impatience and occasional rudeness. The patience we practice will grease the wheels and make for a much more peaceful and pleasant ride.

No Free Ride

*If you are going to play the game
properly, you'd better know the rules.*

Barbara Jordan

Nothing stays the same. Things either progress or regress. Life is activity, be it physical, mental, or emotional. This is how it was, is, and will be. And the same rules apply no matter what phase of life we happen to be in.

"What goes around, comes around" is a popular saying that is full of truth. We get things back in proportion to what we put in. We have all seen instances where on the surface it certainly looked like a person was getting a free ride. For example, an heir or heiress who inherited the family millions at a very young age might become dissolute, leaving his or her life a total waste. It may have looked like a free ride, but it turned out not to be. The price was very high indeed. No, there really are no free rides, as we seasoned ones learned long ago.

Perhaps it still seems sometimes that it would be nice if a free ride were possible; if we could have strength in our muscles without gruesome exercise; if we could indulge in chocolates to our heart's content and still maintain our proper weight; if we could have a host of friends without being outgoing, joining clubs, or reaching out. But that is not how it works.

So we need to keep in mind the rules in this game of life. No worthwhile, desirable goals or achievements are ever reached by way of a free ride.

Maturity

When I can look Life in the eyes,
Grown calm and very coldly wise,
Life will have given me the Truth,
And taken in exchange—my youth.
                                    Sara Teasdale

Carl Rogers tells us the good life is a process, not a state of being. It is a direction, not a destination. As we look back on our lives, we can see clearly that this is so. But while maturity is, in a sense, a destination, it is not static, but rather ever deepening and developing.

Maturity encompasses coming to grips with reality and seeing things as they are, both pleasant and unpleasant. Maturity relates not necessarily to the number of years lived but rather to the degree of understanding and control attained. There are the immature among us who at seventy or eighty still have temper tantrums, think only of themselves, and are selfish and inconsiderate. Thank Heaven they are the exception and not the rule. These people certainly should not be considered stereotypical, which they sometimes are. They are emotionally still children.

They are to be pitied, just as one might feel pity for a severely physically handicapped person. These people give the rest of us a bad name.

The dictionary defines *maturity* as "a state of full development." We might compare the level we have reached with ripened, mature fruit, as we now enjoy the fullness, the climax of growth—the apex. Another way to think of our maturity is that we have tasted the hot and cold of life and become seasoned.

Moderation

Enough is as good as a feast.
                    John Heywood

Have you noticed lately that there are not as many "feasts" as there used to be? Not as much expectation, not as much excitement, not as many pats on the back, not as many parties, and not as many opportunities for interaction with others?

But just because the "feasting" days are gone is no reason to be sad. There is so very much left for us to enjoy. It is quite enough, really, as John Heywood believed many years ago. The good life does not require an overabundance of everything. Excess can lead to satiation, indifference, and lack of appreciation. Of course, to be deprived of life's necessities such as food and shelter is fatal. Beyond the bare-bones physical necessities, though, there is our need for love. The need for love must never be minimized.

We have all we need. There is a certain amount of pristine pleasure in having less. We can do nicely now without all the extras. Have you not found it to be sort of a revelation that a simpler, no longer hectic lifestyle is quite satisfactory?

Substance versus Style

*What do you suppose will satisfy the soul,
except to walk free and own no superior?*
    Walt Whitman

Everywhere we look—in many television programs, magazine articles, books—we find an
emphasis on style, on surface appeal. Thanks to
television, our elected government officials must focus
on the superficial at the expense of meaningful, vital
matters. Victory often hinges on appearance rather
than ability.

While in the past it may have been like that for
us in our career days—always obliged to play the
game of sophistication and surface relationships—we
can rejoice that all that is behind us now. Our
energies, our thoughts, our time can now be chan-
neled toward the genuine and the authentic. We can
exchange the "rat race" for a more peaceful way of
life. No more entertaining unless we choose to, no
more posturing, no more being compelled to spend our
valuable time being bored silly at dreary gatherings.

Now we have the time and the opportunity to

reach a deeper level. It is said that shallow brooks are noisy and that still water runs deep. We should rejoice that we have passed from the shallow brook to the still water.

Time

*Time, whose tooth gnaws away
everything else, is powerless against truth.*
                                    Thomas H. Huxley

Time is such a stately marcher. It is so evenhanded, playing no favorites. A king receives the same number of hours in his day as does the beggar. Time, like Old Man River, just keeps rolling along. Only twenty-four hours in a good day, and no more or less in a bad day.

Looking back, how could all that time have marched by so quickly? Remember when we were kids, how we thought time was dragging when we were waiting for Christmas, or vacation, or even Friday afternoon? Then in our salad days, the nights with our lovers, life was so full of pleasure we wished the clock could stand still. But it never did. Attitudes toward time vary among societies, countries, and individuals. For example, Big Ben and the changing of the guard at Buckingham Palace are almost religions.

It used to be that the biggest share of our time had to be devoted to earning our livelihood, but those days are gone. However, there need be no wasted days. In truth, the only wasted days are those we might spend in self-pity, resentment, or bitterness. If we choose to spend our time this day in the backyard swing relaxing with a book, that is far from wasting our time. It just boils down to making each day worthwhile to ourselves. Let's use the time we have left and be quite aware of its inestimable value.

Exercise

Making a commitment isn't easy.
Penny Reeves-Goff

The following comments are not for you paragons, you models of perfection, who have faithfully exercised all of your lives. These comments are intended for all the rest of us weak-willed procrastinators who have commenced unnumbered exercise programs throughout the years.

We can no longer use our old familiar excuse of not having enough time. And, anyway, it only takes three to five hours a week. Isn't it interesting that only 30 percent of the population participates in a regular exercise program? Many of us now are limited in the amount and kind of exercise we can do safely. But even stretching exercises will help keep us limber. There is a copyrighted exercise program in San Francisco called "Sittercizer," done entirely while sitting on a chair. Most cities have at least one television exercise program targeted for older folks. The thing to do is to decide on an exercise program and make it a top priority. (There are fringe benefits also, such as less time spent watching television or eating.) Also, be wise and discuss your exercise plan with your doctor, and be realistic. The fitness goals of losing weight, strengthening heart and lungs, firming muscles, and relieving stress are the very worthwhile long-term goals of an exercise program. If it is possible to have a workout partner, it will help the motivation.

Let's do what we can to live a longer, healthier life, not only for ourselves, but so our grandchildren and great-grandchildren will have the opportunity to know us.

Asking Yourself Out

The world, after all, is not Noah's ark;
you don't have to be in pairs to be
allowed in.

Ruth Stein

Being alone really isn't an unnatural state, and there is certainly no reason to feel embarrassed or conspicuous when we eat out alone, attend a movie or play by ourselves, or even travel alone. It just takes some doing and some getting used to. The effort pays off, though.

A good many of us choose confinement in our homes, fearing we will be conspicuous. The truth is that most people are absorbed with their own affairs and pay little attention to the situations of others. Attending a movie is the least traumatic activity to attempt alone. The darkness affords anonymity.

Eating out alone is a little more difficult, but taking a book along gives you something to do between courses. Watch out for the urge to eat too fast, and choose a restaurant that has music. It helps to know that you look your best. Especially because you are alone and a bit apprehensive, you need to be self-confident about your appearance. Even traveling alone is quite common and acceptable these days. If you can plan and execute a vacation trip with an enthusiastic attitude, think of how you have enriched your life. Take names and phone numbers of friends and relatives of friends to contact along the way. If you become homesick, you can always call friends back home. Another good idea is to take along a tape recorder to set down your impressions and experiences. (This lets you talk to yourself without being self-conscious.)

There are many advantages. You can sit where you please, and you are free to leave early if you're bored. It may not be better to be alone, but we don't have to miss out on things because we don't have anyone to go with. We can go alone.

Volunteering

Today I will believe that as I give to the
world, the world will give to me.
                                    Earnest Larsen

There is as much for us to gain as to give when we become involved in volunteer work. There is a vital world of volunteers out there today, open to everyone.

Volunteering not only contributes a great deal economically to the community, but it enriches the volunteer's life, also. It is interesting that today's face of volunteerism is changing. In past years, socialites almost exclusively comprised the volunteer ranks, but today they are swelling with the retired and semiretired. Volunteering is not one-sided. Besides offering a sense of contributing and pleasure, it encourages growth as personal needs are fulfilled. Opportunities to learn new skills and expand social contacts also present themselves. Keeping busy as a volunteer is a meaningful way to deal with grief. Caring about other people helps heal a broken heart. The fact that we are physically and mentally able to be "givers" rather than "receivers" is reason enough to volunteer—in order to express our gratitude that this is so.

Did you know that over one-third of Americans are volunteers in some capacity, and that 44 percent of all people over fifty are so involved, according to a recent survey? When the participants in a survey were asked what older people could do to stay well and improve their health, the majority voted for staying active and having a good mental attitude. Both are attributes of volunteering. The message from all of us older volunteers is that taking on the challenge of continuing personal contribution to our society benefits us as well as others.

Effort

Strive and thrive!
Robert Browning

Everything requires effort. Failure is all that will be achieved without it. At the very least, we will feel better about ourselves just knowing that we tried.

While we all know that our lives narrow or widen in proportion to the amount of effort we put into our days, at times it is no easy thing to keep going with verve and vitality. Unfailing dedication to an active lifestyle (physical or mental) does, at times, require tremendous determination—a determination to have it no other way. Leonardo da Vinci once wrote: "O Lord, thou givest us everything, at the price of an effort." Can you think of any meaningful thing in life you received without effort? If you can, it would be as rare as mail on Sunday.

It might be a good idea before dropping off to sleep each night to give a thought to how much effort we pumped into the day, tangible (such as tasks accomplished) or intangible (for example less judgmental). Then say a little prayer that our effort be sustained and supported.

Forgiveness

And the best thing now is to give
him your forgiveness.

2 Cor. 2:7

Anyone can seek revenge. It takes a magnanimous, generous spirit to grant a pardon.

How difficult it is to truly forgive a grievous hurt, a cruel slight! And yet, what is to be gained by rehashing hurtful happenings, wrongful accusations? Nothing, absolutely nothing! The only thing that happens is that they become more deeply entrenched and painful with the passing of the years. And even if we bury them, they stay there in our subconscious, festering. We really need to get rid of our rancor and our hurt feelings. We need to see if we can't manage to give the other the benefit of the doubt. Maybe the remark was not intended the way we took it, or the action resulted from carelessness or lack of control. It might be possible that some wrongfully interpreted action or word or omission of ours was a contributing factor. Sometimes the bottom line is that we just must consider the source (there are many cripples among us) and let it go.

Like all correct actions, there is everything to gain and nothing to lose in forgiving. What we must keep in mind is that when we forgive those who have offended us, we are not doing it for them, but for ourselves.

Our Outlook

*. . .It is a sort of splendid torch which I
have got hold of for the moment. And I
want to make it burn as bright as possible
before handing it on to future generations.*
George Bernard Shaw

If we think of our lives as "a splendid torch" (and
we are free to think of our lives any way we
choose), we become more dynamic and forceful, less
passive and indifferent. Very few pass their "torch"
on with such enormous recognition as did George
Bernard Shaw, because most torches do not burn
with such intensity. Nevertheless, if each one of us
burns our torch "as bright as possible," it will impact
on those we love and on our progeny.

If we never allow ourselves to give up striving
for new directions, we will find vitality and excitement and a will to live. An example of one with a
dynamic attitude is the veteran actor Paul Newman,
who says this of making movies: "I've a long way to
go. I'm just beginning to learn what this racket is all
about." It's true—with an open mind and a lively
attitude, there will always be new things to learn,
new areas to explore.

It is difficult as the shadows mount, but no one ever said it would be easy. Recognizing that the only real constant is change, we can go forward with a positive attitude. "The world stands out on either side / No wider than the heart is wide," was written by Edna St. Vincent Millay. Our heart is as wide as our outlook; our torch is as bright as we choose to make it.

Parental Respect

Honor thy father and thy mother.
Fifth Commandment

The erosion of parental regard and respect has taken place gradually over the past couple of generations in Western society. But it has occurred practically overnight among today's displaced refugees. One could compare this monumentally rapid change to pushing the fast-forward button on a tape recorder.

It is almost impossible for us to imagine the trauma elderly refugees face. Besides having to turn their backs on the greatest portion of their lives, they are faced with loss of respect. In Asia the elderly were the most important, the figures of authority, the storytellers. Now the grandparents are seen as having no use. At age fifty they felt they "knew Heaven's will." Now they are confronted with constant anxiety—far beyond the anxiety the rest of us feel over the loss of family rank. The refugee dilemma does serve to focus our attention and awareness on the fact that today, any esteem or respect received by us will be for reasons other than how long we have lived.

In all fairness, we must admit that the pendulum had swung too far in former years in the direction of revering the elderly—cruelty, unfairness, and a domineering attitude were not uncommon. None of that, however, was justification for the trend we see today as the pendulum swings in the opposite direction. Utter disregard of and rudeness to older people are so very reprehensible and for civilization such a step backward into the mire.

To reverse this trend, our words and actions must stand on their own. We must be so responsible and admirable that the younger generation's approval and respect will be ensured.

Laughing Matters

*Angels can fly because they take
themselves lightly.*

G. K. Chesterton

Those of us who have managed to keep a twinkle in our eye are the true successes in this life, no matter the size of our bank accounts or the number of medals on our chests. If we have held on to our sense of humor, the grace of easy laughter, and still are finding happiness and passing it on, then we have more than come out even in our lives—we have won!

If we will laugh as much as we can from wherever we are, we can transform our lives and our relationships. It actually works. On television recently, a "Candid Camera" program cited the findings of a clinic in California that if a patient could laugh for half an hour, he could resist his pain for four hours. It turns out that there is a scientific explanation for "laughing so hard he fell off his chair." Since laughter affects us so strongly physically, think what it does for our mental and emotional health!

The world may say, "Wipe that smile off your

face," but we don't have to let life inhibit us. If we laugh, maybe the world will laugh with us. And besides, he who laughs, lasts!

Formerly a Parent,
Now a Friend

*And in the sweetness of friendship let
there be laughter and the sharing of
pleasure.*

Gibran

Our children and, for many of us, even our
grandchildren, are now adults. Roles have
changed, a transition has taken place.

The old rules no longer apply. The need is for a
new, loving adult relationship still built on sensitivity,
understanding, good will, and genuine caring. Moth-
erhood (or fatherhood) does not last a lifetime. We
are no longer the arbitrators, the decision makers, the
judges in our children's lives. Some of us are blind to
the reality of the situation and fail to make the
transition. The changing relationship is not obscure,
but quite obvious. One relationship is replaced by
another in a healthy transition. Parental bonds must
be broken. But this does not imply they are not
replaced by something else. That something else is an
honest, caring friendship based on equality and
respect. None of this is instantaneous; rather, the

foundation is laid by years of unselfish, wise love.

We are now equals, our children and ourselves. If our relationship is to ripen and deepen, it must be with intelligent recognition of what has taken place and a welcoming of the new role, which in no way needs to be less significant or pleasurable.

Depression

*I am not responsible for my feelings, but
what I do with them.*

Hugh Prather

Severe clinical depression is an illness demanding
expert medical attention and is not the subject of
reflection here. What is referred to are mild feelings
of depression, the "blues," despondency that hits all
of us at times.

It is impossible to avoid these feelings entirely,
but it is possible to refuse to allow them to overpower
us (except in the case of mental illness). These feelings
tell us that something is not right in our lives and
that we need to correct it, whether it is physical,
psychological, or social. With mild depression we are
pessimistic and sad, feel worthless, and lose interest
in our activities. Thorough physical examinations on
a regular basis are necessary to discover incipient
health problems. Then we must look at psychological
(mental attitude) and social (relationships) aspects.
Many are helped immeasurably by a competent,
understanding therapist. Also, there are support
groups to help overcome feelings of isolation that
sometimes present themselves after retirement.

Talking to a friend about how we feel, helping someone else, or finding things to do that give us pleasure are wise routes to follow.

A despairing outlook is not inevitable and need be only fleeting. We must realize that feeling depressed is not irreversible—that we can deal with it and dispatch it. These feelings are a part of life and will pass if we crowd them out with the positive.

Individuals, Every One!

To each his own.
Proverb

Gerontologists have learned that those over sixty-five are more different from each other physically, mentally, and emotionally than are the members of any other age group. Millions of people over sixty-five are living in varied stages of health, disability, and happiness.

Some of us are so fit we can participate in marathons, swim in icy waters, compete in (and win) other forms of athletic competition. At the other end of the spectrum are those stricken with Alzheimer's disease and other brain dysfunctions. In between are all gradations of human activity, from the feeble to the robust. It probably should be no surprise that we are the most varied group in society, since we are the most experienced and have had more time to become what we are today.

The old stereotype of the elderly as helpless and hopeless is no more. It has now been replaced. The fact is that today there can be no stereotype for us because there is just too much individuality. Each one of us is unique, living out our lives in our own fashion.

Self-Assessment

All your life you feel the same age.
Tolstoy

There are two ways of looking at ourselves as we grow older. One is denial—refusal to accept that our time on Earth is becoming shorter and shorter. The other is a realistic acceptance. They are both means of coping.

There are those who refuse to admit to themselves or anyone else that they are now in the elderly age group. These people refuse to belong to senior citizen groups or take advantage of senior discounts. The men often have long hair, unbuttoned shirts, and lots of gold chains. The women risk broken legs in their high heels, dress conspicuously, and wear an overabundance of makeup. They cope by denying.

The rest of us see and accept that one door has closed, but that another has been opened for us. Julia Child, the gourmet cook, says it well: "If you pretend old age is not going to happen, it will fall right on you. Facing up to old age can help you be at peace with yourself." Although at times we may feel like the man who said, "A golden-ager? The golden years, they say. Maybe they mistake rust for gold," that thought passes. If we are living honestly, we know that to a great degree we are responsible for our own successful aging.

Taking a hard, intelligent look at ourselves—at our frame of mind as well as our daily activities—will help us stay on the road of happy living for years to come. Aim to be one of the Elegant Elderly.

What Is Success?

To laugh often and much; to win the
respect of intelligent people and the
affection of children; to earn the
appreciation of honest critics and endure
the betrayal of false friends; to appreciate
beauty; to find the best in others; to leave
the world a bit better, whether by a
healthy child, a garden patch or a
redeemed social condition; to know even
one life has breathed easier because you
lived. This is to have succeeded.

Ralph Waldo Emerson

In our Western society, too often all that comes to mind when we hear the word *success* is "lots of money," "a fat bank account," "valuable possessions," "riches." We must not use these criteria when we evaluate our lives. They signify less than nothing.

The person who has grown old but never lost life's zest is a success, even if he doesn't have a dime. The person who is stiff, hurting, and fatigued but remains cheerful is a success. The shy, withdrawn person who with great effort attends the weekly senior citizen program is a success. Those who strive at activities that are purposeful and meaningful are successful. Those who can lower their expectations but find greater satisfactions have succeeded.

Those who never fail to be kind have succeeded. All of these people have done more than exist. They have lived well, and lived successfully.

Remaining Vital

I would rather be ashes than dust, I would rather my spark should burn out in a brilliant blaze, Than it should be stifled in dry rot.

Jack London

The professional football quarterback, Ken Stabler, was asked what Jack London's poem meant. He gave the perfect explanation when he said, "Throw deep!" Some time spent thinking about this can charge us up.

The sound of the words "stifling in dry rot" is enough to get us off any physical or mental dead center we may have slipped into. We have seen "dry rot" people among our family members, our acquaintances. We have seen it among those not yet in the last quarter of their lives, too, which is even sadder, if possible. Those who not only fail to "throw deep" but who fumble and drop the ball have lost the art of living. When the game is over they will not have won, or have even come out even. They will have lost.

As we work our way through life, not chance

but choice is what will keep us vital. We need to take a fresh look at our perspective every morning, determine to maintain a freshness of outlook, and continue to "throw deep."

Class

*Many persons strive for high ideals; And
everywhere life is full of heroism . . . In
the noisy confusion of life keep peace with
your soul.*

Desiderata

We observe class when we see an ordinary person
forging on when he has every reason and right
to give up or crack up. A person with true class aims
at sharing instead of hoarding, and caring instead of
flaunting. He or she tries to do more than go the
distance. A hallmark of class is the automatic tendency to rejoice at another's achievement or good
fortune.

Class is laughing when we feel like crying,
getting up when life knocks us down, refusing to
accept defeat, and forgiving those who hurt us. The
dictionary says that one of the meanings of *class* is
"high quality"—in other words, a degree of excel-
lence. There are vastly different ways to react to a
situation or a problem—nobly or ignobly, with
courage or cringing. In other words, with class or
with no class. There is a choice.

We all have opportunities to act with class in meeting the demands of the day—for patience, humor, endurance, self-sacrifice, understanding, forgiveness, and bravery. Class may well be nothing else but the ability to face the trials and tribulations of life with love and hope and a light heart. Ultimately, class may be being old, bent, and battered, but nevertheless waltzing off the dance floor, waving gracefully, and maybe even throwing the world a kiss or two.

Endings

Grow old along with me! The best is yet to be, The last of life, for which the first was made. Our times are in his hands.
Robert Browning

Just as it seems incredible that the world was viable and vital before we were born—the sun rising and setting every day for thousands and thousands of years when we weren't here to see it—it's also hard to believe that it will manage without us someday. But it will.

We will have left our minute marks on the world, and most of us will also leave our contribution to the gene pool in the form of our progeny. And one day we will move on, consumed by that unfathomable thing called life.

We have observed all our lives that when one door closes, another seems to open. Why should this not still be our experience—an ending leading to a beginning? Contemplating this, many emotions present themselves—wonder, anticipation, sadness at leaving, some apprehension of the unknown, and some natural resistance to the inevitable.

From now till then we must reaffirm our conviction

that our lives have counted for something, have had meaning. We must know in our hearts our lives have mattered. We will not just have fallen from the race. We will have *won*! And gone on to "the best that is yet to be."

Individuality

The shoe that fits one person pinches another; there is no recipe for living that suits all cases.

Carl Jung

It is quite easy to become intimidated reading the accounts of seniors living exciting, daring lives—climbing mountains, breaking swimming records, performing feats of strength. Sometimes we feel guilty (ah, that fiend *guilt* still raises its head) that we have chosen to withdraw from the competition and the struggle to win, win, win!

We are all so different. Our needs are so varied. Our stamina and health run the gamut from excellent to poor. Our lifestyles are certainly diversified. So why set up models for ourselves to emulate?

Read of these people with passing interest, not with envy or a feeling of inferiority. That is how they are working out their lives and this is how we are working out ours. Neither is the better way—only the better way for *us*. It is all so relative anyway. The shy introvert who forces herself to go to the senior center every week is as admirable as the athlete who wins a medal in some competition or other.

How to Be Happy

*Find something bigger than yourself and
throw yourself away on it, if you want to
be happy. There are takers enough on this
vexed planet.*

John Neihardt

As we grow older, our worst temptation is to
become self-absorbed, and that is the shortest
path to misery and unhappiness. Along this route
personality shrivels and friends disappear.

It was said long ago that "If I lose myself I find
myself." This is a fundamental truth that we have
read and heard through the years. We need to
reaffirm its meaning. Today, getting the most out of
life often means acquiring money, houses, cars,
jewels. At this time in our lives, we get our heads on
straighter and see more clearly that "enough is almost
too much of everything but sympathy," as Neihardt
put it.

Of course, we need to care for ourselves. But
beyond that, happiness can only be found in dedication
to others, in worthwhile achievements, in contributing
to that which is beautiful, in promoting harmony.

Money doesn't care who has it or what is done with it. It is people who care, people who matter.

Even now, in retirement, we can all be givers—even if we give only a smile. It is no small thing.

Love Yourself

I take care of me. I am the only one
I've got.

Groucho Marx

Being less than we once were is not cause for despair. So we don't walk as fast, we have wrinkles, we now need glasses and hearing aids. Even though we may be slightly bent and going forward may seem impossible, always remember that it is too soon to quit.

A trip down disaster lane is no way to go. Even if Ponce de Leon got the last bottle at the Fountain of Youth, we need not despair. We still have ourselves, and we count. Never forget it! It has been said by many different people in many different ways that it is impossible to love others if we don't love ourselves. And, of course, that is true. It follows, then, that we take care of who or what we love, starting with ourselves. This includes physically (healthy living, medical care), emotionally, and spiritually.

So even if energy lags and beauty fades, we must be faithful to ourselves. As Shakespeare said, "Who can say more than this rich praise, that you alone are you."

Grieving

*Grieving is believing in the Beauty of what
we've known with the Love we've shared
together out of a faith made desperate
through absence!*

Bill Larsen

The emptiness remaining after the death of a loved one is so crushing that words fail. Mental suffering and distress are overwhelming. And yet the sun does shine again. Never quite so brightly, but it does reappear from behind those black and dreary clouds when we are ready to look up.

So even if our laughing years are gone, what remains can be a time of acceptance and contentment, a time of new challenges and caring and hope. "Aimer est souffrir," the French say—"To love is to suffer." The pain of losing a loved one is the price we pay for having had that love.

The mystic chords of memory will forever be ours. Here is the last verse of the poem quoted above:

"So, we grieve (as need it be) relentlessly holding to the memory of what is lost, Lovingly and with pride, whetting with our tears the cost of having paired Essences until, eventually, (pain's lesson realized) we see that NOTHING ever changes save the simple presence of whom we've loved so dearly."

A Lively Spirit

Whatsoever thy hand finds to do, do it with thy might.

Eccles. 9:10

If we want to be among the all-time winners, we are going to have to continue to live our lives with enthusiasm—no letting down. The temptation to give in to frailty and pain is often intense and almost overpowering.

All our successes throughout our lives have been obtained by our unfailing effort. And now, maybe even more so, it will see us through. It takes force of will to maintain equilibrium through all the changes that are occurring in our lives. A determination to give each challenge, each project, each activity our best effort is what will motivate us to keep on going.

Many years ago, when the twentieth century and all of us were young, our energy bubbled over and our "might" was more than enough. It is somewhat harder to come by these days. But that only means the challenge is greater, and so also will be the reward.

It has been said that great works are performed not by strength but by perseverance.

Goal-Setting

You can't turn back the clock, but you can wind it up again.

Bonnie Prudden

It is so very easy to fall into a passive way of life. All of us retired folks are very susceptible to becoming couch potatoes. Heaven forbid! To avoid such a fate, we must fuel the fire that makes our old engines go.

Recognizing the problem and setting goals to keep active, interested, and interesting is the fuel that is needed. Personal goal-setting and the pursuit of those goals on a regular basis are an important process for maintaining a viable lifestyle and for resisting deterioration. We need to set goals to give us direction and help provide some order to our lives. Some of us have activities, roles, and responsibilities that give structure to our lives and are not in need of specific goal-setting. But for others, that which gave structure is gone for one reason or another. This may lead to a loss of direction and purpose, and to helplessness and inactivity.

When trying to set goals, it is best to start with a short-term daily one—to go for a walk, to call or write a friend. What really counts is perseverance. It is helpful to set goals with others. Working toward a shared goal gives us feedback, support, and encouragement. We have gotten along very well with life so far, and there is no reason to change that now.

If we make up our minds we can't do it, we are absolutely right!

Spice It Up!

There must be a spice of mischief and
willfulness thrown into the cup of our
existence to give it sharp taste and
sparkling color.

William Hazlitt

Abraham Lincoln once said, "Whatever you are, be a good one." No one can argue that that is not good advice. It is advice we probably offered our children when they were growing up and can now repeat for our grandchildren. We can also repeat it to ourselves and heed it.

Now that we are the older generation, we can collectively be a *good* generation. To be a *good* older person requires staying alive and interested in what is going on around us. Not always easy anymore, is it? The sourpusses give the rest of us a bad name.

Nobody ever said life would be easy. As we have discovered through the years, successful living takes enormous effort, and that requirement certainly hasn't lessened, has it?

Be Satisfied

Ask for a lot, but take what is offered.
Russian proverb

So very much unhappiness comes from craving what we don't have. It seems to be human nature to always want more.

Happy and at peace are those who recognize that what matters is what is in their heart. Bemoaning getting older is such a waste. Age is important only when choosing wine or cheese. So life has knocked the corners off us—that's how it is. There is still so very much left!

Life is precious! Gifts abound! Those of us who take all our blessings for granted—blessings that are ample to sustain and nourish us—are, in effect, eating our seed corn. There is nothing but emptiness left to sustain us in the days to come.

Happiness comes only to those who are aware of their blessings, and it eludes all who are unappreciative and discontented.

As an Irish proverb tells us, "The trout in the pot is better than the salmon in the sea."

Realism

Drop the question what tomorrow will bring and count as profit every day that Fate allows you.

Horace

Is our determination to continue on despite the difficulties foolhardy? No, it is being realistic. Life demands such a quality in abundance from us, with no letup.

From season to season, we have always taken our chances each day with no assurance of any refuge. Whenever life yields another terrible surprise, we are flooded with fear, gloom, and despair. How could it be otherwise? Repeated blows and unexpected losses take their toll. Even the hardiest of us sometimes must realize that our only choice is to change course. But this is not giving up. The spirit still refuses to give in.

When a salamander loses a limb, it grows a new one. An oyster makes a pearl around an irritation. Remember that we deserve the space we stand in, and there is no reason to panic—the future is something everyone reaches at the rate of sixty minutes an hour—whatever he does, whoever he is.

Zest

May you live all the days of your life.
                    Jonathan Swift

Blessed are those who wake up looking forward to the day ahead. No matter whether what is to come is delightful or dreadful, *how* it is faced is the key to successful living.

The word *enthusiasm* comes from the Latin *en* and *Theos*, meaning "from God." Norman Vincent Peale has written, "Hold on to your enthusiasm. It's a gift from God." What a tremendous gift to face life with hearty enjoyment and gusto. The alternatives— indifference and boredom—are so negative and destructive of mental and physical well-being.

It is a good idea to take a look at our lives daily for signs of negativism. Like all habits, good or bad, success comes with repeated actions—in other words, with practice. Looking forward to each new day is a no-lose attitude.

Malcolm Ford says it well: "People who never get carried away should be."

Just Be There

The limitation of death clouds all human aspirations.

Geddes MacGregor

At those sad times when our friends have suffered the loss of dear ones, we often feel helpless and awkward and don't know what to say or do. We recall the times when we have been in similar situations and have had to endure thoughtless and unfeeling remarks from insensitive people. We recoil from the possibility of doing or saying anything that would put us in that category.

We need to at least tell our friends we are sorry this has happened. We can ask if they want to talk about it. To let them know they are not alone and can share this tragedy with us is a kind gesture. To expect people suffering a heartfelt loss to just shove their feelings under the rug, as we do in this country, only intensifies the suffering.

In some European countries, mourning is recognized and black arm bands are worn. In those countries it is not necessary to wear a mask (as is expected of us), and grieving is permitted to come out of the shadows.

If we just are there, we will have helped.

Lighten Up

It is easy to be heavy; hard to be light.
G. K. Chesterton

Often these days we are threatened with some pretty dreary possibilities, and a little humor helps us deal with these unexpected burdens and frustrations. Maybe it is really only whistling in the dark, but that is a darn good way to walk through those scary shadows.

When life deals us low blows, the best way to fight back, to refuse defeat, is to "whistle"—to maintain an optimistic outlook. The way to spell relief from pain and disappointments is to purposely take a deep breath and lighten up. The "juice" can still flow. Refuse to allow it to dry up. Ellen Glasgow said, "No life is so hard that you can't make it easier by the way you take it." And there are many documented cases of those with terminal diseases who got well when their lifestyle and attitude changed.

We can change. We must use our minds to improve the quality of our lives. A light spirit is a defense mechanism. It wards off disaster. Try to see the joke in everything. It is a saver for all of us.

A sense of humor is the ultimate therapy.

Priorities

Slow down so you can go faster.
Ken Blanchard

As we travel the uncharted terrain of the rest of our lives, it is no doubt a good idea to reassess our priorities. Maybe it is time to revise our thoughts about what is really important.

Now, more than ever, is the time for balance. It is the time to strengthen our inner peace, to realize that being, not having, is what counts. As our bodies become less efficient, our minds can continue to develop. All our lives, time has been of the essence. Finally we have the time to read, to develop new friends, to travel, and even just to *think*.

All these things are available to us when we get our priorities straight. Maybe the time has come to give up the forty-hour (or more) workweek. Maybe we should cut the size of the garden in half. Maybe the house can get by with less than everyday cleaning. Maybe a great portion of that time-consuming cooking can be replaced by eating out more often or by using some of the excellent prepared foods at the market these days.

Get those priorities straight! Something good will come out of it!

Growth

*The purpose of learning is growth, and
our minds, unlike our bodies, can
continue growing as we continue to live.*
                              Mortimer Adler

It seems like forever since we were in a school classroom situation—at least, for most of us. But, of course, that is only one facet of learning.

Our times, like never before, offer ample and various opportunities for learning. The spectrum is almost limitless. The only way we can possibly miss out is because our minds are closed to new ideas. Individually or in a group, we can pursue knowledge that intrigues us. How many times in the past have we said: "If only there was time to read about that," or "Someday I'll take a course in that." Well, someday is here.

So don't get comfortable in a rut. Get going. New ideas are more precious than gold and will give our outlook a boost, which we need at times.

Look for encounters of the learning kind!

Winning

You have to expect to win, because if you don't you already have lost.

Ricky Hunley

The words above are about the game of football, but this wise comment can be applied to all of life's contests and challenges.

No matter how spectacularly and cruelly we are felled, getting back up is what is impressive. We can handle our setbacks and grow from them when we refuse to accept defeat. This is not to glibly say that it is easy—it seems that everything we do takes more effort these days. However, once we accept the reality of the way things are, we will be winners if we maintain our good humor and give our best each day.

Winners are those who have a song of gratitude for life in their hearts. They make life better for themselves and every life they touch.

Fear

*Do the things you fear, and the death of
fear is certain.*

Ralph Waldo Emerson

We can all recall times in our youth when fear
and dread of disaster just about wiped us out—
the fear of having to give a talk in front of the class,
the fear of facing the anger of our folks when we had
disobeyed, the dread of asking a girl to the prom. So
many times, all through our lives, we have been
awash in fear.

Fear is a miserable state in which to be. And,
after all these years, we are still gripped with it at
times. There really is no way to attack fear but to
face it. There is no pretending it is not there. That is
diversionary and only temporary. The only way to
get rid of it is to do the thing you fear and march
right through it.

Overcoming fear allows us to do more than just
survive. It allows us to live fully.

Haven't you found that often what you feared
has turned out to be nothing you couldn't handle?

Stand Up and Be Counted

Death isn't failure. Not living is.
Dr. Bernie Siegel

It certainly is not easy to maintain inner strength and be determined to live a productive life. There are many facets of productivity. It is simply not true that once a paycheck is no longer coming in, all contribution to society has ceased. Far from it!

Of course, those who allow themselves to become couch potatoes may be breathing, but are they living? Even if the legs have succumbed to the ravages of time, the mind hasn't. Never lose sight of that. There is a treasure of earnest wisdom that has increased through the years. As life goes on, it is a mistake to "fold our tents and quietly steal away" when we have so much to offer and life has so much to offer us.

"If you can't flow, flee." That's a current glib expression. The couch potatoes have chosen not to "flow" but to be among those who have chosen to flee—to withdraw from life.

Freedom of choice! That's a great gift we have. Choose to live!

Alone in the Crowd

It's a surprise how lonely this land (old age) feels, even though there are so many others traveling here.

Ella Rausch

Even though John Donne's beautiful poem says that no man is an island, each of us probably has experienced, at times, an overwhelming feeling of floating alone into the unknown. Thoughts and expectations often become confusing and bewildering.

Awareness of our mortality grows sharper with the passing years. How could it be otherwise? Often we find ourselves the only one in the family group who has reached retirement. The others are busily engaged with raising children and with career demands, just as we were in time gone by. Salvation lies in sharing and caring with friends, old and new, who are now at the same point on their journey as we find ourselves.

Getting old can be tough to swallow. Reaching out, sharing feelings with one another, resisting isolation—those are the elements that will help us avoid feeling alone in the crowd. They will act like steel cables, powerfully offering us security and much needed encouragement.

Positive Thinking

*Positive thinking is the glue that binds the
loose ends of our lives and keeps us from
falling apart.*

Darrell Sifford

More and more evidence is piling up for the
importance of a positive mental outlook. Positive thinking enhances all aspects of our lives,
including our physical well-being.

The importance of a positive mental outlook
before surgery is recognized by many surgeons today.
It is believed that if the patient thinks he is going to
die, there is an increased chance that he will. We
need to keep in mind the importance of our mental
outlook, not only before surgery, but all the time.

It is believed that negativism tends to put to
sleep the body's natural disease fighters and encourages all kinds of terrible things to happen, including
cancer. On the other hand, it is likely that a positive
attitude can revive the defense mechanism and not
only throw up a protective shield, but battle disease
already present and sometimes wipe it out.

If we can convince ourselves that we are what we think and rid ourselves of all phases of negativism, our lives will be greatly enhanced. What do you think?

American poet Louise Bogan said it well:

"I cannot believe that the unscrutable universe turns on an axis of suffering; surely the strange beauty of the world must somewhere rest on pure joy."

Adjusting

The best human being is the one who adjusts best to the changing circumstances of life.

Peter Taylor

Living involves constant role changes. Our first role change was from our mother's womb to living in the world, breathing and receiving nourishment on our own. What an adjustment that was! And adjusting to change has been part of our existence ever since.

Being left by our mothers at nursery school was a big one. No longer being the baby when the new little one came along was traumatic. So many adjustments through the years—from grade school to high school to college, and then working and marriage and children! And many other adjustments in between—some pleasant and some not so pleasant. But we always responded with the necessary fortitude and grace, somehow.

Nothing has changed, not even change. We are still faced with the necessity of adjusting as we continue on life's path. And, as previously, successful living is achieved through skillful adjustment—through awareness, acceptance, and adaptation. It is foolish to waste valuable time fighting the inevitable. Successful living demands adjusting to the changing circumstances of life.

As long as routine dictates the pattern of living, new dimensions will not emerge.

Dare to Dream

Whatever you can do—or dream you can—begin it. Boldness has genius, power, and magic in it.

Goethe

Whenever the thought, "Wouldn't it be nice if. . . ?" comes to us, let's not sigh and discard it. If it is a fanciful thought like, "If I were only sixteen again," we know that is not to be? But what of other thoughts of things that could be. Maybe all we need is to go for it.

Every new door we open now, every new venture we attempt, no matter how scary or daring or seemingly insignificant, enhances our lives. Even without great success, as judged by the world, we will have the satisfaction of knowing we gave it a try. We must remember, too, that as Dr. Samuel Johnson said, "Nothing will ever be attempted if all possible objections must first be overcome." It is not enough to have ideas about what we would *like* to do. It is not enough to talk about taking aim—we have to pull the trigger.

As Carl Sandburg said, "Nothing happens unless first a dream." No matter how small or how momentous our ideas might be, all that matters is that we act boldly and put them into action. "Alas for those who never sing, but die with all their music in them," said Oliver Wendell Holmes. We must not let our songs die, ever.

We Were There!

*I am not afraid of tomorrow, for I have
seen yesterday and I love today.*
William Allen White

The changes we have witnessed during our lifetimes are fascinating to discuss among ourselves
and with our children and grandchildren. There have
been more changes in the last fifty or seventy-five
years than ever in man's history.

Here are some items once quite common. You
can, no doubt, think of as many more:

trolley cars with a motorman
    and a conductor
horse-drawn delivery wagons
goose grease and turpentine
isinglass for car windows
first flight across the Atlantic
airplane in the sky a novelty
coal furnaces in basements
wood stoves
iceboxes
cloth diapers
gaslights
long underwear
cranks to start
    cars
sweet spirits of
    niter
castor oil
housecalls by
    doctors
wind-up gramophone
bathtub stopper
silk hose with seams
clotheslines

A list of the things we have now that were
scarcely dreamed of in our youth would be even

longer. Yes, our world has certainly changed, and we should be exceedingly proud of ourselves for being open and alert to all of it.

Time can't rob us of our memories. They are forever.

Stress Level

*We all have an optimum level of stress—
the amount we can handle well.*

Dr. Rod Martin

Each one of us has always had our own level of stress tolerance. Some of us thrive on high levels; others are quite the opposite. But it seems that all of us have lower stress levels than we did in years gone by.

Life's unexpected glitches are more stressful now for a number of reasons—some methods of coping are no longer available to us, physical limitations are often aggravations, and we are playing in a different ballpark. Where we used to thrive on excitement and change, we now seek the absence of pressure. Research on those with coronary heart disease indicates that mental stress can disrupt blood flow to the heart, contributing to heart disease and heart attacks.

The fact that there probably is a direct link between stress and heart attacks is good reason to avoid it. Some stresses we cannot avoid, but we do have the power to control our reactions. Fermenting thoughts cause physical illness. We must sift out the unimportant. As Confucius put it: "Men stumble over molehills, not mountains."

When we are aware of our need to reduce stress in our lives, we are then in a position to do something to control it. The first step is realizing there is a problem and accurately evaluating it.

Laugh Therapy

Laughter is a massage from the inside out.
                                    Anonymous

Have you noticed how laughter breaks down barriers? Speakers commence their talks with a funny story almost without fail. Tense situations and stalemates can often be broken up with the introduction of a little humor. There are no unsolvable problems in families that laugh together.

Laughter is good for the body as well as the soul. It gives it a quick burst of circulation-improving exercise. Lila Green, of the American Association for Therapeutic Humor, calls laughing "inner jogging." It releases endorphins—natural painkillers. Research points to the fact that a positive outlook is beneficial in fighting off disease.

Maybe we should think about bringing joke books to a hospitalized friend, instead of flowers. And sharing a laugh may be our best defense against illness. It certainly improves the quality of life.

Why take up space with anything but good cheer?

A Sense of Meaning

*We have to be conscious of our own part
in life, however modest, to be genuinely
happy. Only then can we live in peace
and die in peace.*

George Roche

These are the reflective years for most of us. There is more time now to meditate and attempt to put the pieces of our lives together. A sense of meaning finally gives the point to life and death.

What seems to count, from the vantage point of advancing years, is that we lived our lives without begging off. Since we were invited to the feast, we have participated with as much grace, gusto, and enthusiasm as we had the ability to offer. To know that each of our lives is an important part of the whole is the answer to the cry of our hearts for meaning.

Knowing that we are all part of the universe will give us stability and courage.

Normal Aging?

*To use the word "normal" in describing
certain age-related declines in function
implies they are harmless, that they
cannot and should not be changed.*

Dr. John W. Rowe

It is good that there is a trend these days to separate
the effects of aging from the effects of the many
diseases that tend to beset older people. It is also
recognized that other factors, such as habit, exercise,
nutrition, and even personality traits and economic
status, greatly affect the aging process.

A differentiation needs to be made between
usual aging and successful aging. The person aging in
the usual way finds his or her habits and environment
increasingly aggravating and frustrating. In contrast,
those who age successfully are able to work out a
lifestyle that enables them to cope well with the
changes that advancing years bring.

It becomes apparent that successful aging is more
than physiological. To quote Dr. Rowe: "There's
satisfaction, there's function, there's resilience; they

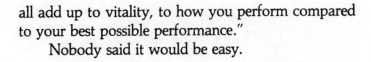

all add up to vitality, to how you perform compared to your best possible performance."

Nobody said it would be easy.

Young in Spirit

*He who strives thus to mingle
youthfulness and age may grow old in
body, but old in spirit he will never grow.*
Cicero

It is an interesting fact that most of us picture ourselves as we were in our adult prime. In our mind's eye, we do not see an old person. Then why do we so often limit ourselves with negative assessments of our appearance and ability?

A youthful spirit requires optimism and flexibility. Being open to change and not resisting new approaches is the key to youthfulness. While it is not easy, it *is* possible, if we try, to enjoy even our grandchildren's loud rock 'n' roll music. There was a time long ago when the older generation even thought Bing Crosby's music was horrendous and sinful.

Disliking and criticizing all that is new is negative. As youth-oriented as our society now is, it is important that we resist becoming crusty old curmudgeons.

Few better will come after us if "old in spirit we will never grow."

Widowers

Wealth lost—something lost;
honor lost— much lost;
courage lost—all lost.

Old German proverb

The death of a spouse is the most traumatic thing one can experience. It brings enormous stress and men in particular find it extremely difficult because they are relunctant to talk about their feelings and to ask for help. They sometimes become involved in auto accidents, commit suicide, or neglect their health to the point of early death. It is a fact that newly widowed men are more or less ignored and forgotten. The truth is that they need help through the grief process every bit as much as widows do.

There are organizations now, such as the Widowed Person's Service of the American Association of Retired Persons (AARP), which are experiencing success with outreach programs for widowers. Widowers are invited to attend men-only breakfasts and luncheon "socials." There they learn about the program and meet other men facing identical loses.

Grief and personal problems are not discussed at these meetings. If a widower chooses to join the group, one-on-one outreach follows. It is a great concept, and many can be helped if they become involved.

Cheerfulness

Everyone likes a happy story.
Henry McDowell

There are none more welcome in this world than those with a light touch—those who are calm, relaxed, and pleasant. There is no need to envy such people. The thing to do is enjoy and emulate them.

One of the many reasons children are such a delight is their bubbly approach to whatever is going on. There are few, if any, sounds more delightful than children's laughter. Too bad those days unclouded by any doubts and worries pass so swiftly. But life goes on, and our parades are often rained on. There doesn't seem to be any correlation between cheerfulness and how hard the rain is falling. Many times the most cheerful individuals are getting the worst of the storm, while those walking in the sunshine are doing more than their share of the complaining.

A cheerful way of life, of facing each day, can never be anything but a win/win approach. Cheerfulness is a habit, and like all habits, it can be improved and strengthened. When we make cheerfulness a way of life, we not only improve our physical and mental health, but brighten the lives of others. We must have our light side to survive with some balance.

Keeping Busy

*To do nothing except kill time is not
murder, but suicide.*

> Dr. M. Scott Peck

Just because the possibilities are no longer endless is no reason to let ourselves become stale and dull. Life goes on. That's the name of the game, and the successful game plan calls for not giving up.

Those who wake up already bored before they even open their eyes need to take control of their lives. Louis Auchincloss had a wise comment on this subject: "The only thing that keeps a man going is energy. And what is energy but liking life?" If we are going to like life, we must continue liking ourselves. Bored people are really boring. If we allow ourselves to become bored by a lifestyle where we are just killing time, we lose our energy and our will to live, and then we have really lost the battle.

Willie Shoemaker, probably the best jockey who ever rode a horse, is now in his late fifties and still riding winners (even in the Kentucky Derby). He may be in the twilight of his life, but he is living it like he was in the dawn. Of course, most of us can

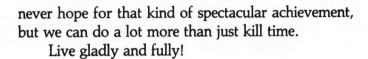

never hope for that kind of spectacular achievement, but we can do a lot more than just kill time.

Live gladly and fully!

Friends

Old friends go away, one way or another.
New friends come along when we give
them a chance.

Anonymous

Life's changing patterns wreak havoc on our store of friends. If we have the opportunity to look back at old Christmas card lists, birthday reminder notebooks, or photograph albums, it becomes quite apparent that many old friends have gone away, one way or another. For those we have lost through death, Saint-Exupery said it so poignantly: ". . .then come other years when time does its work and our plantation is made sparse and thin. One by one, our comrades slip away, depriving us of their shade."

But that is life, and we must cope as best we can with courage and insight. Now is the time to make new friends. And they *will* come along if we give them a chance. We need to be consciously aware of our need and be open to making new friends. The easy way is to cocoon, but this will lead to an ever-narrowing life.

Friendliness can be a lifesaver. Reach out! Be friendly!

What's Important

*A good name is rather to be chosen than
great riches, and loving favored rather
than silver and gold.*

Prov. 22:1

Just a little reflection on the above verifies its truth.
Wealth overflowing (think of Howard Hughes's last
years) is a meaningless substitute for the happiness
and satisfaction of a life lived in love and with peace
of mind.

Few of us have ever had more money than we
knew what to do with, but perhaps that was a
blessing. It is quite possible that we could have had
more money in the bank now, be living more
grandly, if we had been willing to cut corners, profit
from shady deals, treat others ruthlessly. Even though
today's society encourages cheating and distrust at
every level, it does so at its own peril.

This world would be much better if it could be
said that there was never any harm in anyone, or
violence, or greed. The truly rich among us, no
matter the size of their bank accounts, are those
whose hearts are filled with love.

Courtesy

*Life is not so short but that there is time
for courtesy.*

Ralph Waldo Emerson

Have you noticed lately a faint glimmer of the
return to recognizing the importance of courtesy?
The current advertising campaign of one of our
leading department stores emphasizes the courtesy of
their salespeople. What a breath of fresh air in these
times that have nearly buried politeness and good
manners.

While courtesy in the marketplace is certainly to
be desired and really gives the edge in many compet-
itive situations, it acts in our private relationships as
a hassle-reducer. Rudeness begets hostility. As Prov-
erbs 15:1 tells us, "A mild answer turns away wrath,
sharp words stir up anger." Families that are cour-
teous to one another stay together.

It has been said that the time is always right to
do what is right. It is difficult to conceive of a time
when courtesy would not be a beneficial approach in
any human interaction between sane people.

Physical Pain

We can approach pain as a victim or as a gallant fighter.

Merle Shain

Many of us of late have had to learn to live with miserable, excruciating pain. Of course, pain tolerance differs and the experience is subjective. Nevertheless, it is unpleasantly distracting at any level.

If we allow ourselves to become victims of pain, all is lost. Being a victim means giving up and giving in to pain. When we do that, pain rules and dominates our thinking, ruining any chance of a normal life. And allowing pain to overcome us creates a vicious circle that intensifies our suffering. When learning to live with pain, we sometimes look back and try to remember (without success) what life was like before. Regardless, this is what has happened to us while we were making other plans, and we are now confronted with the problem of how to best live with it.

If we can envision ourselves as gallant fighters (rather than victims), our coping will be more successful and we can avoid the miasma of despair. In addition to a brave spirit and faith in our Higher

Power, gallant fighters need to fortify themselves with all the ammunition available, such as good nutrition and appropriate exercise, support groups, and interests outside themselves.

When the wind has quit blowing, it is time to start rowing!

The Time Is Now!

We must not waste life in devising means.
It is better to plan less and do more.
William Ellery Channing

Now is the time to do the things that will keep our hearts singing. It has been wisely said that we should never regret the things we have tried and failed—only the things we have failed to try.

If you've often thought you could write a novel, why not give it a try? If you have played around in the past with the idea of going back to school, there are ways to accomplish that, and not necessarily by attending classes on a campus, either. There are television classes for credit as well as courses by mail. Maybe you have said that when you had time you would learn to sew, or to play bridge, or to grow prize roses. Now is the time to start doing!

Maybe there is buried talent that we have not as yet discovered. Life's treasures are to be developed and used and enjoyed. No matter if the talent is minor, it will enhance your life immeasurably. Lost time is lost forever.

It's All in How You Take It

*Life is 10 percent what you make it, and
90 percent how you take it.*

Irving Berlin

In a very real sense, we all have in us the will to
survive, if only we don't submerge it in despair and
self-pity. Acknowledging that our salad days are gone
and facing up to today's reality with courage and
hope is true maturity.

How futile it is to wallow in depression because
we are no longer as physically attractive as we once
were, or because our bodies are not as resilient as
they used to be. Life can always be meaningful if we
choose to have it so.

The further we travel into old age, the more
challenges we face, and we become aware that we
are equipped to handle them (often to our surprise).
When we take life as it comes, thorns and all, we
have become wise and valiant.

As Amelia Earhart Putnam said, "Courage is the
price that life exacts for granting peace."

Growing Old Gracefully

I don't intend to grow old gracefully.
I intend to fight it every step of the way.
                                    TV commercial

If the cosmetics people have their way, maybe we won't ever have to grow old—gracefully or any other way. They make growing old sound like a horrendous calamity rather than just a natural occurrence.

With the addition of Retin-A to remove wrinkles and Minoxidil for the bald to the already enormous supply of elixirs on the market, the choices being offered are phenomenal. Cosmetic surgery now even includes liposuction for middle-age spread. It seems we are limited in our choices only by our ability to pay or our concept of what is important.

It all depends on our attitude about growing older. But doesn't it seem rather futile to chase after youth? Self-hate needs to be replaced by self-acceptance and self-esteem. Let our pride in our youthful good looks be replaced by pride in our maturity and accomplishments.

Age is a matter of mind. If you don't mind, it doesn't matter.

Apathy

*A choice confronts us. Shall we, as we feel
our foundations shaking, withdraw in
anxiety and panic? Frightened by the loss
of our familiar mooring places, shall we
become paralyzed and cover our inaction
with apathy?*

Rollo May

Throughout our lives there have always been
options at each fork in the road—some momentous and some trivial, but nonetheless always there.
Nothing has changed. We still have options.

Biologically, of course, we have no choice but
to grow older. Even that inevitability can be slowed
by wise health habits. Where our actual choices lie
are in the control of our own minds and attitudes. It
will pay enormous dividends to be alert to narrowing
interests—an inclination to throw in the towel, so to
speak. Let the red flags go up when we notice that
we are becoming unconcerned and disinterested in
what is going on around us. Apathy is attacking!

In his writing concerning apathy, Rollo May
says: "If we do those things, we will have surrendered
our chance to participate in the forming of the future.

We will have forfeited the distinctive characteristic of human beings; namely, to influence our evolution through our own awareness."

The antidote to apathy is caring. Refuse to "withdraw in anxiety and panic."

Open-Ended Possibilities

They can because they think they can.
Virgil

Who is to say what possibilities lie ahead? However, as an old Irish proverb says, "You'll never plow a field by turning it over in your mind."

Fear of failure brought on by lack of confidence is a major factor that holds us back from trying something new, like writing our memoirs. Many of us have wonderful memories of the past and family stories that go back to the Civil War and often much further. When we are gone, all that will be lost. What a pity! Apathy is another of our enemies. It takes effort and desire and determination to learn something new, to try a different way of doing something, but the rewards abound!

We are the instrument of our own destiny. New ideas bring personal growth. While we are living, there is no reason to ever stop growing.

New ideas, thoughts, and plans are most often as evanescent as a whispering wind. Seize them—don't let them get away.

Kindness

Kind words are a honeycomb, sweet to the taste, wholesome to the body.

Prov. 16:24

Kindness can be thought of as on a continuum. At one end is politeness (not hurting another's feelings) all the way to agape (a self-giving concern that freely accepts another and seeks his good).

To witness acts of kindness is to restore our faith in mankind. This world is so full of greed and self-aggrandizement, kindness sometimes seems hard to find, but it is all around. To watch a small, barefoot child picking up an even younger, also barefoot, sibling to carry him across a hot sidewalk is to observe true kindness. Those who volunteer their time to help others in so many different programs are practicing true kindness. Offering to ease another's load, whether it be giving up a seat on the bus or visiting a prison, is to contribute to the advancement of civilization.

There are so many ways to be kind. Refraining from putting someone down, either to his face or behind his back, is an act of kindness. An old Irish proverb goes like this: "A silent mouth is sweet to hear." Sensitivity is a form of kindness. Caring enough about others to be aware of their feelings and to act accordingly makes for a kind individual.

A good rule of life is always to try to be a little kinder than is necessary.

Stagnation

Don't let a guidepost become a hitching post.

Fortune cookie

The saying that when one door closes, another opens is familiar to all of us. That statement should be amended to say, "Another door opens *if* we open it."

As these later years toss us around, there is a tendency to grab a tree branch and hold on. It is tempting to stay there and try no more to reach a safer, more dependable anchor. Sure, we can sit safely in our homes and experience the light of life going out, but we don't have to do so. Life has dumped on many of us so cruelly that it is easy to understand why we become satisfied with only a tree branch to cling to.

The interesting thing, though, is that there is no correlation between the amount of dumping and the heroism in living life fully. It is the difference between surviving and overcoming. Often those showing the most fortitude and willingness to fight are those fate has treated most harshly.

A handsome reward is offered to those who keep moving on.

Recharging the Batteries

*Getting old is something it is not too easy
to do heroically.*

Ashleigh Brilliant

There comes a time when our enthusiasm and joy in life begin to wane. We have had many losses, much pain and trauma. When our inner resources are strained and we feel like dry sponges, it is time for us to seek replenishment.

A Higher Power has sustained us through many problems and adversities in the past and will always be there for us. Some resources that helped us weather the storms in the past are no longer available to us. Pressures that we are under now take their toll on our physical health as well as our mental health. Our thinking and feeling become impaired. Guard against those feelings of monotony and joylessness.

We need to be in contact with our Higher Power, asking for help in finding new avenues of enthusiasm and in confronting our problems wisely and with vigor. Joy can be found in self-renewal.

Peace of Mind

*There's no need to fear the wind if your
haystacks are tied down.*

Irish proverb

The concept of peace is truly beautiful. The anto-
nyms of peace are war and contention, the fruits of
which are pain, misery, and unhappiness. Peace, however, brings harmony, love, and joy. We, who have
lived through many national as well as personal wars,
know well their horror and the glory of peace.

Having "your haystacks tied down" is the clever
Irish way of expressing the thought of having made
peace with life. It's a coming to terms with who we
are and what we are. It is understanding and
acceptance. To reach this summit may have taken us
approximately the time needed to build the pyramids,
but no matter—we have found tranquility and we
are winners.

"Worry makes the heart heavy," we read in Prov.
12:25. There is no place for worry and fear in us if we
have peace of mind. There is strength within ourselves.

There is no need to fear the wind anymore—we
are safe and sound, our inner, God-given strength
tied securely.

Habits

*Whatever you would make habitual,
practice it; and if you would not make a
thing habitual, do not practice it, but
accustom yourself to something else.*

                                        Epictetus

It is never too late to acquire habits, both good and bad. Can you not think of an older relative who picked up a habit of drumming on the table or speaking too loudly or mumbling? Some become very argumentative who were never quarrelsome in their earlier life. Others, formerly outgoing, become reclusive. And so it goes.

What a shame that it is so insidiously easy to slip into bad habits. It truly bears vigilence if we are to experience a graceful old age. As the above quote says so truly, "If you would not make a thing habitual, do not practice it." Since positive approaches are so much more effective than negative ones, acquiring good habits will save the day.

As much as possible, get in the habit of being seen at your best at all times. Often we are like the boy in Abraham Lincoln's story who stubbed his toe and said, "It hurts too much to laugh and I'm too old to cry." But we can at least get in the habit of smiling, if we practice.

Practice how not to be a difficult person. It will put truth into the old Irish proverb: "The older the fiddle, the sweeter the tune."

Character

During my eighty-seven years I have witnessed a whole succession of technological revolutions. But none of them has done away with the need for character in the individual or the ability to think.

Bernard M. Baruch

The more things change, the more they stay the same. Around the unknown curve, what awaits our civilization technologically is unimaginable. But the world's need for people with character and comprehension and caring will never change.

We are not through making our mark upon the world. We are needed now to light the way. Now is our time to communicate to those coming up behind us the value and desirability of kindness, patience, loyalty, and integrity. It is our responsibility to pass on to the next generation what we have learned of life. Now, when integrity battles temptation and despair, is our golden hour.

Our ability to think and reflect on life is what leads to wisdom. This is above and beyond formal learning. Joan Erikson, wife of psychoanalyst Erik Erikson, believes real wisdom "comes from life experience, well digested." This is what we have to contribute to our society.

Each Day Counts

*If we take care of the inches we will not
have to worry about the miles.*

Hartley Coleridge

One of the Alcoholics Anonymous slogans is, "One day at a time." This wise thought reminds us to live our lives with the knowledge of the importance of each day, but without undue concern for what is to come. The downbeat maxim, "Sufficient unto the day is the evil thereof," is a pessimistic way of expressing the same idea of living in the present.

What matters now is what we do with the days we have left. Material wealth is not a requisite for a happy life. It can even be a hindrance to peace of mind, as expressed in the saying, "A man with a watch knows what time it is. A man with two watches isn't so sure." When we live each day facing the future with courage and the hours with good humor, we have succeeded.

Even if life no longer grants us freedom from pain, the challenge of living fearlessly day by day is only intensified. Each day lived well makes the next day easier. When we review the day, we are reminded how well or poorly we took care of the inches and avoided worrying about the miles.

Death and Dying

Death is an absolute natural necessity in the scheme of things.

Sigmund Freud

We must move on to make room for future generations when our lives have been exhausted. Bodily immortality is not for us.

In our society, with its emphasis on youth and pleasure, the phenomenon of death tends to be ignored and hidden as much as possible. Lately, however, the concept of hospices has been a step in the right direction. But for the most part, the terminally ill, aged person is still isolated because of our culture's bias. It would be good if we would return to the bygone practice of grandparents teaching the younger generation how to live and being allowed to die at home with the support of the family.

A survivor of the Lusitania sinking (May 7, 1915) reported that a passenger, Charles Froman, said these last words to a group of friends: "Why fear death? Death is only a beautiful adventure." Could there be a more hopeful and serene attitude on death than that?

C. S. Lewis, in his book about his wife's death (*A Grief Observed*), says that he has "a sense that some shattering and disarming simplicity is the real answer. . . . We cannot understand the resurrection of the body. The best is perhaps what we understand the least. . . . How wicked it would be, if we could, to call the dead back! She said not to me, but to the chaplain, 'I am at peace with God.' She smiled, but not at me."

Helen Hunt Jackson wrote meaningfully of dying in the following lines: "Oh, write of me, not 'Died in bitter pains,' But 'Emigrated to another star!'"

We Are More
Than Just Our Bodies

God has called us to a life of peace.
1 Cor. 7:16

There are those who would disagree with the title above—the atheists. That is their choice. How desperate growing old must be for them! How bitter "the despair that gradual physical disintegration can too easily bring," as Erik Erikson writes.

That despair is not for us. Rather, let us join with John Quincy Adams as he responded to a question concerning his well-being on his eightieth birthday:

"John Quincy Adams is well. But the house in which he lives at present is becoming dilapidated. It is tottering upon its foundations. Time and the seasons have nearly destroyed it. Its roof is pretty well worn out. Its walls are much shattered and it trembles with every wind. I think John Quincy Adams will have to move out of it soon. But he himself is quite well, quite well."

When we have fully integrated into our belief

system the thought that there is much more to each one of us than just our bodies, then we can become impervious to the disappointments and frustrations that beset us. We rise above them, as John Quincy Adams did.

Believe in the integrity of the soul.

We Need Each Other

Fragrant oil gladdens the heart,
friendship's sweetness comforts the soul.

Prov. 27:9

Jean-Paul Sartre once wrote, "Hell is other people." So caustic a statement is shocking, but, of course, that is why he wrote those words. While we all have come across people who were boring, and some even nasty, they have been the exception, thank the gods!

We all need some solitude and quiet time in our lives, but more than that, we need each other. Erica Jong's flip statement that "solitude is un-American" has some truth in it, as sometimes the insignificant chatter that bombards us seems unending. However, above and beyond the noisy prattle, we all need a shoulder to lay our deepest cares on. In spite of, or because of, our vulnerability, it is more vital than ever that we recognize and accept our need for human contact, for friends.

We must open up and reach out to one another in a spirit of friendship. "You cannot shake hands with a closed fist," said Indira Gandhi. What we give to others we get back in one way or another, over and over.

May we all have good friends with whom to share warm words on cold nights!

Best Defense? A Good Offense

In youth we run into difficulties; in old age difficulties run into us.

Anonymous

Difficulties run into us? Boy, do they ever! Since it cannot be denied that growing older brings many difficulties with it, the question is how to defend ourselves.

Cringing in the corner, waiting for disaster, is cowardly. Pretending we are still middle-aged and need not be concerned with growing older is dishonest. The first step in preparing a good offense against old age is knowing and admitting to ourselves that we are vulnerable, that we are faced with potentially severe problems. If we attack these problems now, we can handle them before it is too late for us to do so.

A good offensive starts with a firm reliance on our Higher Power for sustenance. An Irish proverb says, "It's no use carrying an umbrella if your shoes are wet." Starting out with "dry shoes," we can then proceed with our attack by aggressively retaining a zeal for life and an indomitable spirit. It is important that we take care of ourselves mentally, physically, and psychologically. If we do this, our offensive will succeed.

Crying

*Crying opens the lungs, washes the
countenance, exercises the eyes, and
softens down the temper, so cry away.*
                                  Charles Dickens

Crying in response to what we are feeling is a
natural physical process. We should not be
ashamed of it.

While crying is a natural human emotion, it is
by far one of the most misunderstood. Mostly we
feel that crying is a sign of weakness, of being out of
control, or of immaturity. It has recently been
discovered that there are actually two kinds of tears,
differing in their chemical makeup. There are tears
caused by irritants in our eyes (peeling onions is a
good example) and emotional tears, which actually
contain more of a substance our bodies produce
when we are under stress. Since tears are helpful both
physically and emotionally, what a shame it is that
our society frowns on crying, especially for men.
Maybe that attitude contributes to men having a
higher rate of stress-related illnesses than women.

There are healthy reasons for tears. They can
help somewhat when we are in physical pain, too.

Crying in response to what we are feeling is a natural physical process and a release. We need not be ashamed of it.

It is neither necessary nor healthy to always fight off our tears.

Role-Changing

We are no longer safe in the bosom of the majority.

Anonymous

"Time is a dressmaker specializing in alterations," wrote Faith Baldwin. In retirement, we are learning a great deal about alterations, that's for sure.

Life is a continuum, with children at one end and all of us over sixty-fivers at the other. The long stretch in between is the "majority." The children are much too young and immature to be aware of the situation, but we are not. There are daily encounters to remind us. The ruthless advance of time relieves us of the responsibility of choice. The thought that no one escapes old age (other than those who die young) is of small comfort.

Maintaining the conviction of our intrinsic worth will be a help in gracefully accepting our new role. Take some comfort in the fact that the sixty-five-and-older population has grown twice as fast as the rest of our population since the early 1960s. The U.S.

Census Bureau predicts that by the year 2030, one-fifth of all Americans will be over sixty-five.

Circle the wagons! We can defend ourselves against the arrows of remorseless change.

Chronic Pain

Out of suffering have emerged the
strongest souls, the most massive
characters are seared with scars.

                                        E. H. Chapin

It is a mistake to expect others to understand exactly what we are experiencing when we live with chronic pain. There probably is nothing more personal. Most of us are lucky enough to have family and friends who are concerned, but beyond that we are on our own to endure the best we can.

Living with chronic pain takes a great deal of strength, never ending, day in and day out, without letup. It is a constant battle. We must deal with anger, resentment, frustration, all negative feelings. Eventually, as we learn to deal with these feelings and overcome them, we get a sense of accomplishment and self-respect. Nobody ever said it would be easy to live with chronic pain, and it isn't. In fact, it is probably the hardest thing we ever had to deal with.

There is great solace in prayer. "You can survive the heat if you are prayer conditioned," said a church bulletin. Finding a support group can be helpful, also. We gain strength from one another. The bottom line? Keep trying, and when you feel you haven't the strength, still keep trying. Heroism is inseparable from suffering.

It takes force of will to beat pain. We must focus our minds away from the pain and seek those things that will cause us to laugh through our tears.

The Best Medicine

Frame your mind to mirth and merriment,
which bar thousand harms and lengthens
life.

William Shakespeare

Even as long ago as Old Testament days it was an accepted belief that humor could help keep us healthy. Recently it has been proven scientifically.

In a book entitled *The Laughter Prescription*, the authors, Laurence Peter and Bill Dana, say, "Aches and pains can intensify if attention is given them. A degree of anesthesia can be achieved simply by drawing attention from the pain. At least for the moment, the laughing person pays little attention to the source of discomfort."

Laughter does make a difference to our bodies; it reduces tension. It stimulates hormones secreted by the adrenal glands, which causes increased alertness and a greater sense of well-being. This is not to imply that laughter is a cure-all, but it is definitely a powerful tool in staying well.

Fear of Growing Older

*It is necessary for us to "name" our fears,
to come to understand them, and to enter
fearlessly inside them in order to win
freedom from them.*

Malcolm Boyd

We have all occasionally been assailed by fears ever since we were very small. Childhood fears can be devastating—fear of the dark, fear of monsters, fear of a neighborhood bully, fear of the dentist. Most of these were resolved early on, thank goodness. But few of us are completely free of all fear.

The fear of growing old is the fear that tortures many of us now. As each decade of our lives has ticked by, we have felt a twinge. There was a tug when we realized we were no longer in our twenties—a certain something was gone forever. We had to bolster ourselves a bit for forty, and fifty pushed us to the edge of our self-confidence. Beyond sixty, we often tend to panic.

We can take the sting out of our fear of growing old if we refuse to be its victims. When we overcome the fear of growing old we can hang on to our self-esteem. We are on a journey—there is no going back even if we wanted to. This is new territory to be explored and investigated and lived. It is up to us to make the most of today in every way we can devise.

Peace

*Face the winds and walk the Good Road
to the day of Quiet.*

John Neihardt

The bottom line for us is to strive for peace of mind. We need not be frightened by darkness outside, but by the darkness inside ourselves. If we cannot find peace within ourselves, we can never find it outside.

When we choose not to want what we cannot have (in other words, to accept where and who we are), to look forward, not back, we will experience harmony in our lives. Other cultures recognize the beauty and value of peace of mind. A tribe in Liberia says, "My heart sits down." Natives along the Ivory Coast call peace of mind "a body song." Elsewhere in Africa, locals say, "Where the still waters run."

We must rid ourselves of old hurts and forgive as best we can. As the Irish say, there is no use in boiling your cabbage twice. Ambition, which has driven many of us so hard for so many years, can finally be expelled. Prov. 30:8, which says, "Give me neither poverty nor riches, grant me only my share of bread to eat," directs us to a life of tranquility. Eradicate fear. It sometimes carries us farther than courage, but in a different direction. Wisdom and peace of mind go hand in hand. They are synonymous. If we "face the winds" with courage, peace of mind will be ours.

The Ripple Effect

*Ultimately, all you can do is fix yourself.
And that's a lot, because if you can fix
yourself, it has a ripple effect.*

Rob Reiner

There is a paradox here. The more we try to improve our own shortcomings, the better the effect we will have on others—especially those we care for most deeply. The saying that values are not taught but caught can be extended to attitudes and actions.

If a little self-assessment reveals that we are becoming narrow and resistant to new ideas, it is time to take heed. We must not allow ourselves to become like those people about whom William L. Phelps was talking when he said: "At a certain age some people's minds close up; they live on their intellectual fat." If we notice symptoms of withdrawal—not attending group functions, lack of interest in what is going on around us, less involvement in our friends' lives—it is time to move from that track to one that is going somewhere besides downhill to deterioration.

Whatever we do to "fix" ourselves (as Rob Reiner says) is, in fact, the only way to help our friends "fix" themselves. Shifting our efforts into high gear will not only propel us upward and onward, but also show the way to others.

All things come to he who waits, but they come sooner if he goes out to see what's wrong.

Confidence

*To be successful you have to believe that
you are every bit as good as anyone else.
You have the ingredients to be successful if
you have the desire. Believe that you can
be a winner. Do not lose your confidence.*
Donald Petersen, Chief Executive Officer
Ford Motor Corporation

Of course, the above quote was not directed to retirees, but we can certainly apply this counsel to our present life situation. Successful living in retirement requires the same skill that guided us when we were younger.

If for one moment we allow the thought to enter our minds that we have become inferior to those younger than we are, we have become guilty of self-betrayal. Sometimes we may need to dig deep for the ingredients to keep us from losing heart. *Our desire to be successful at growing older is the linchpin that holds us together.*

There is no reason now to lose the confidence that has seen us through our challenging lives. We are still winners—we are a survivor generation. Joe Namath said it well: "If you are not going all the way, why go at all?"

Confidence will see us all the way!

Living Longer and Better

To know how to grow old is the master
work of wisdom and one of the most
difficult chapters in the great art of living.
                                            Henri Amiel

We go after what we want now, as we always have. Extending our lives is what we are after, but with the important qualification that we want those added years to be quality years.

Personal satisfaction and happiness until the end is a goal worth pursuing. We know that we cannot stop the clock, but we certainly can slow it down. A great deal of current research today is aimed at unlocking the mysteries of the aging process. It is becoming apparent that aging, in itself, is not the body's worst enemy. It is disease that harms the heart. Probably the greatest aid in keeping fit is exercise. It is the closest thing we have to a Fountain of Youth. Exercise contributes to intellectual competence, too. What greater benefit could there be?

Everything doesn't change as we grow older. We are definitely still the same people we always were.

Everything doesn't decline: in fact, more things stay the same than change. A great deal (probably at least 50 percent) depends on how we take care of ourselves. So let's keep on trying to live longer and better.

Improving the quality of our lives will make us feel better and will ensure maintenance of our autonomy, which is so critical.

Who Is Successful?

Anything you're good at contributes to happiness.

Bertrand Russell

Did you ever try to figure out who has success? Are you successful? Observing the lives of the rich and famous leads us to the conclusion that they are no happier than we are. So what is success, anyway?

Reflection reveals there are many levels to it. If it is equated with accumulating vast amounts of money, then those who make the Fortune 500 are successes. But if happiness is the criterion, then those five hundred do not necessarily qualify. If athletic prowess is what is required to be considered successful, then most of us fail. If making the cover of *Time* magazine is success, few will be considered for the title.

What needs to be recognized here is that success is not to be judged by society. True success is not in the amount of money we have or the trophies we've won or the fame we've achieved. True success is self-administered. It comes from deep inside a person who knows that he or she did the best possible, with selflessness, love, and courage.

They are successful who do all they can to keep a healthy distance from things mean and hateful.

A Force in the Marketplace

Advertisers rethink campaigns to cash in on "senior boom."

It isn't always easy these days to find things to bolster our sometimes faltering egos. With such emphasis on youth-related matters in our society, it is not difficult to fall prey to a sense of unimportance.

But there is a change blowing in the wind. Corporations are becoming aware that many older people have money—some, lots of it—and that they are enjoying what it can buy.

Television has brought some of this recognition about. Formerly, you seldom saw older people on television, and when you did they were in wheelchairs, or otherwise in sad shape. All that is changing now. Think of the many popular older actors we have. We are becoming visible as people realize that we compose a huge, lucrative market. The statistics are revealing: one-third of all personal income in the United States is found in households headed by people fifty-five and over. And Americans over the

<c

— 222 —

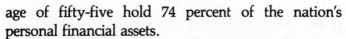

age of fifty-five hold 74 percent of the nation's personal financial assets.

Realizing our power in the marketplace fortifies our sense of well-being and importance.

Discontent

What makes us so discontented with our condition is the absurd, exaggerated idea we have of the happiness of others.

Anonymous

The grass generally does look greener on the other side of the fence, doesn't it? Why should that be?

"Insecurity can mean lack of self-knowledge," says Hugh Prather. It has been said that if we were allowed to trade our troubles with someone else, chances are we would choose to keep our own. However, observing others' lives, we are often misled. The couple we envy because they are apparently so devoted to one another indeed may be. Then again, their personal relationship may be much more shallow and less satisfactory than ours. The person always talking about how devoted her children are to her may be devastatingly lonely and neglected. The rich and famous, who apparently have it all, may be lacking in some of the things that make our lives abundant.

The truth is we are made rich by what we give. And we all have the ability to give. There is no need to envy those whom we perceive to be full of truth, beauty, goodness, and love. These are gifts for the taking. Be observant. Be aware of the necessity to look beneath the surface.

Rather than discontent, let loving and accepting be our motivating force.

A Matter of Choice

People who work in intensive care know there are worse things than death.

Mark Rosen,
Mount Sinai Medical Center, New York

It is only recently that public attention has begun to focus on the question of people's right to make their own decision about when it is time to remove life supports. While euthanasia is illegal and unacceptable to all but a few in our society at this time, the issue of withholding or withdrawing life-prolonging treatment is less clear.

It is interesting that a survey of two thousand people recently showed that 90 percent believed adults who were competent to make decisions should have the right to refuse life-support measures, even over the objections of family and doctors. Court decisions have confirmed this right. Also, 70 percent thought the immediate family, not the courts, should make such decisions on behalf of comatose patients. We have all heard of people in comas with incurable diseases being kept alive at great cost and suffering to the patients and also their families, sometimes for many months or years. Can there be any justification for this?

Here are five modern techniques that are used to prolong life: cardiopulmonary resuscitation, mechanical ventilation (takes over lung function), renal dialysis, artificial feeding, and antibiotics. Except for the antibiotics, none of the above techniques can cure an illness—they only prolong life. There are choices.

Speaking Out

To see the right and not to do it is cowardice.

Confucius

The more things change, the more they stay the same. To see the right and do it is a goal of honest people throughout their lives. That is the ideal. The reality is that the goal is not always reached, unfortunately.

It becomes easier to escape our responsibilities to ourselves, as well as others, by thinking, "Let someone else do it." It also is not difficult to fall into a mindset that says, "I've done my share; let someone else do it now." But sincere reflection tells us that we are never off the hook when it comes to responsible living.

As long as we are able, we must continue to pay our dues. Let the record show that we, the older generation, continue to do what is right with all the courage we can muster.

Self-Confidence

To be happy, we must not be too
concerned with others.
                                        Albert Camus

At this point in our lives we have certainly earned the right to please ourselves. Of course, it is a given that we must not allow our actions to disrupt or cause harm to others, but with that one limitation, we should feel free to cultivate our own happiness.

Before we are all felled by time, we must fill each day with what makes *us* happy, not what we think someone else has decided will make us happy. If others look askance at our pleasure in watching the birds or the sunset or whatever, be not disturbed. Simple does not translate to stupid. Simplicity is as far from stupidity as love is from indifference.

Old habits are hard to break, but if we become aware that our lives are being inhibited by concern over what someone else might think of us, it is time to reorganize our perceptions of what is important. Really, we need only to please ourselves to be *happy*.

Impatient Patients

*Avoid doctors whose offices have lots of
waiting rooms!*

Linda Shrieves

"People are becoming less sheeplike and less in
awe of physicians, so they are no longer
accepting those inconveniences as a necessity of
medicine," said Arthur Levin, of the Center for
Medical Consumers, discussing the common practice
of overbooking by doctors. There is no situation
today, other than in a doctor's office, where we are
expected to wait an hour, sometimes more, beyond our
appointment time. Not even being told that there will
be a delay or given an apology adds salt to the wound.

Those of us who have gotten up and left after
an hour of waiting had a questionable victory,
inasmuch as our problem was unaddressed and was
still with us. Even writing a letter of protest only
salves the ego a little. There are two reasons why this
problem is coming to the forefront: people are just
too busy these days—their time is too valuable—and
doctors are being viewed more as businessmen and

peers than gods too sacrosanct to question. So, even if we retirees have more time at our disposal, we, too, would like to use it doing something other than reading old magazines while time ticks by.

Here are two good suggestions: try to get the first appointment in the morning or one right after lunch, or call ahead to ask if the doctor is running on time.

Physicians are people, not deities. Don't be a passive recipient of inconsiderate behavior.

Adapt We Must!

The sand shifts, it doesn't blow away.

Anonymous

The image of our lives changing, becoming quieter, is quite dismaying to those of us who have been dynamic all of our lives. Gail Sheehy, well-known author, has this to say on the subject: "Changes in life are not only possible and predictable, but to deny them is to be an accomplice to one's own unnecessary vegetation." The fear of being trapped in a dull and vapid life for years to come is very real.

There really is nothing to threaten us so or cause us anxiety in contemplating this change in our lives. Once we recognize and accept that everyone is in a state of flux, we can make peace with the inevitability of change. We must be alert to the benefits, just as we were when other inevitable changes occurred in our lives: starting school meant new friends, going to college meant freedom from supervision, being employed meant independence, etc. Now, the quieter life of retirement gives us more personal freedom. Distractions and conflicts are reduced.

The key to successful living now is tied up in allowing our lifetime of experience to lead us on a slightly different path. Quieter, yes, but deeper, too.

The sand shifts but is still there, only in a different pattern.

Plant Your Own Garden

*Decorate your own soul instead of waiting
for someone to bring you flowers.*
Ronnie Shoffstall

As children we leaned on our parents, depending on them to direct us, to make plans for us, to provide guidance. If our parents were wise, they gradually encouraged us to strike out on our own, and eventually we became autonomous and independent.

However, as we grow older, there creeps in a tendency to wait for someone else to enrich our lives, to plan our recreation, to alleviate our loneliness. It is such a mistake to go this route. It only leads to us becoming burdens, which is exactly what we don't want to happen. We need to always be open and looking for our own opportunities. It really is sad to try to carry on a conversation with someone living in the past. Just marking time until your life is over serves no purpose.

We can all have the sense of our stock going up, not bottoming out, if we never stop "decorating our own souls." Self-respect requires that we carry our own weight.

William Blake said, "No bird soars too high, if he soars with his own wings." Keep those wings beating!

Some Things Are Better Forgotten

For life goes not backward nor tarries with yesterday.

Kahlil Gibran

There is probably no one who would not agree that self-torture is about as inane as it gets. And yet, at times we let old humiliations, mistakes of poor judgment, painful hurts come back to haunt us.

Times when our pride was reduced to ashes need not be dwelt on. Slights that wounded us deeply at the time perhaps were not even intended, and, even if they were, we survived them. We, who have had many ups and downs in our lifetimes, know that life can be very cruel sometimes. What a waste to spend our precious time on painful memories.

We need to refuse to allow our minds to dwell on the tortuous memories. Live for today. Hang on to an upbeat attitude.

We can survive living with painful memories, but we are not living fully.

Be Open to New Ideas

*The foolish and the dead never change
their opinions.*

James R. Lowe

The wishy-washy individual who flits from one faddish approach to life to the next is not to be admired, of course. But neither is the person who refuses to consider any new approach, anything the least bit different, any new evidence.

No generation, at least of recent memory, has ever been assailed with so much change. Those whose minds are set in stone, patterned after their parents' mindset, aren't likely to reassess their opinions. An example of how harmful this can be is the repulsiveness of prejudice. Even after we have recognized the wrongness of such an attitude and determined to free our thoughts of it, traces still rear their ugly heads from time to time. Life should be a long learning process, and we have failed to keep it so if we close our minds to new ideas.

It takes a good deal of thought, investigation, and openness to change a long-held opinion. Yes, humility, too. And on things not frivolous, as an ancient proverb says, we must "measure a thousand times and cut once." One wants to be as sure as possible he has chosen wisely.

Our Significant Others

Wherever you are it is your friends who make your world.

William James

Those people in our lives whom we hold in high regard and who return our feelings, who are mutually supportive and caring, are our significant others. They are our friends, related to us by blood or desire.

A friend is one who wishes us well. A friend is one to whom we are truly attached by feelings of affection and concern. A friend causes our eyes to light up when we meet. A friend's telephone call makes our voice have a lilt in it. A friend is supportive. In our lifetime, we can only have a few significant others. Maybe that is one reason they are so precious. How very colorless our lives would be without them!

Hundreds and hundreds of years ago, in ancient Rome, Cicero wrote of friendship. Here is an excerpt from his essay: "How can there be a life worth living . . . unless it rests upon the mutual love of friends?

What could be finer than to have someone to whom you may speak as freely as to yourself?"

Here is a comment by Lillian Hellman concerning significant others: "In the end they were together for the best of all possible reasons: the sheer pleasure of each other's company." That pretty much says it all!

Endurance

*Patience is a virtue that carries
a lot of wait.*

Anonymous

It seems there is a certain amount of stoicism that needs to be developed as the "hands of time sweep us toward the twilight of our lives." Of course, no one should be so stoic that he or she represses all emotion.

Rather, we need to develop a calm fortitude. Patience, strength of character, and courage are what it takes to prevail against disappointment, pain, and trials. So, under the trying circumstances that often engulf us, what will see us through is our own stability and persistent courage. We are called to exercise patience in many ways—with ourselves, with others, with circumstances beyond our control. All of us can no doubt recall some impatient person we have known—someone with such a short fuse that we felt we were walking on eggs when in his or her company. There was no control there, no peace, and little maturity.

Don't believe that calm fortitude is a mission impossible. Let the record show that, through our patience and our ungrudging endurance, we chose the best path.

Did you know that the sugar maple isn't tapped until it is sixty years old? There is a good example of patience paying off!

A Sense of Humor

Humor helps, and a sense of proportion. I am one individual on a small planet in a little solar system in one of the galaxies.

Roberto Assagioli

The very best way to bolster our staying power is by never losing our sense of humor. The ability to see the funny side of life's trials is not a gift. It is an ability available to anyone willing to lighten up.

It is all too easy to fall into the bad habit of a pessimistic outlook. Just reading the morning paper is enough to ruin our day if we let it. Heaven knows there is enough pain and loss to justify gloom, but that is a given. Why dwell on it and allow our enjoyment of life to be ruined? No, by far the best approach is to refuse to allow the negative to take over, and to accentuate the positive. Be open to the comical—it is all around us if we look for it. Being honestly aware of our own foibles is a good source of humor-producing thoughts.

A line in the song "It's a Small World" says, ". . .a smile means friendship to everyone." Smiles are free, so why not give them away? Indulge ourselves. The Bible says, in Prov. 15:13, "A glad heart means a happy face: where the heart is sad the spirit is broken."

Winning Battles

*Until the day of his death, no man can be
sure of his courage.*

Jean Anouilh

It may be true, as Dostoevski wrote, that the only
battle that counts is the last one, but that does not
take into account all the little victories that make that
last one possible. It has been going on all of our lives.

Facing up to life all along the way, scorning
alibis and excuses, living each day bravely, are the
things that assure victory at the end. It is easy to slip
into self-pity and to continuously complain. If that
happens, then courage is gone and there will be only
lost battles.

Human dignity and individual values are what
will keep us on the right course. There is no deus ex
machina to lift us out of our tribulations—only our
own perseverance and determination.

We are stronger than we think. Our rivers run
deep!

Optimism

Our greatest glory consists not in never failing, but in rising every time we may fall.

Oliver Goldsmith

When you think about it, isn't it downright ridiculous to make ourselves depressed and gloomy? Defeats and setbacks are part of life. Sometimes we have to go through hell to get to heaven.

But why make situations more difficult than they need to be through our own miserable attitude? Life goes on and we do what we have to do, which isn't letting despair overcome us. It isn't possible to always have a blissful feeling (though that would be lovely), but it is possible to refrain from crepe-hanging. Many of our worst worries never materialize. How much wiser to expect the best. It is a proven fact that such an attitude is good for us physically, too.

The more we practice looking at the bright side and expecting the best, the more optimistic we will become. We need to adjust our mental emotional thermostat from "blue" to "rosy."

We never lose what we always use. So keep those spirits, if not soaring, at least upbeat.

At the Head of the Line

White hairs are a crown of honor.
Prov. 16:31

It seems such a short time ago that we were way at the back of the line. We all can remember those days when we were lowly freshmen in high school and college. There was a time when we were the youngest in the office, the youngest teacher in the school, the youngest recruit in the platoon. Yes, there was a time when we were preceded in line by almost everyone. There was no "back" to look back to.

No more! No longer is anyone ahead of us in the line of life. While looking back in memory is a rich source of pleasure for us, we are still able to look forward with anticipation. However, if we do either to excess, we are cheating ourselves by robbing ourselves of today. All any of us have for sure, whether we are young or old, is the present—the right now.

We must not let the precious present be unappreciated and unenjoyed because we pushed it into the future or let it slide into the past. Time passes all too quickly as it is.

A minicourse in enjoying the present would benefit us all.

Slowing Down?

*Don't fear going slowly. Fear only
standing still.*

Chinese proverb

Have you noticed lately that it is taking us a little longer than it used to to do things? Often the young people have finished their dinner when we are only halfway through ours. We are a little poky getting in and out of the car. We used to walk a mile in less than fifteen minutes, but not anymore. We used to get to the phone on the first or second ring, but now our friends know to let it ring seven or eight times.

Slowing a bit is the nature of things—unavoidable and to be expected and accepted. However, we must avoid slowing to a stop, to stagnation. The really great thing is that our minds don't slow down. Almost all of us are as intelligent in old age as we were in youth. In fact, ten percent of the seventy-four to eight-one-year-olds in a two-decade study by the University of Southern California performed better in mental tests than they had at younger ages.

As long as the slowing down process does not affect our ability to think and use our minds, it is not too difficult to accept, and can actually be a pleasant, restful change from all the scurrying and rushing.

A Happy Heart

*There is nothing either good or bad, but
thinking makes it so.*

William Shakespeare

The unconscious is powerful, and when we allow
an undercurrent of subversive thoughts to infil-
trate our minds and our outlook, we are dialing "D"
for disaster. Bad things happen all too often, but we
don't drown by falling into the water. If we drown,
it is because we didn't struggle and get out.

A good way to determine if our heart is glad is
to determine whether we see our glass as half full or
half empty. If we can manage to get into the habit of
seeing things half full, our lives can be much happier.
Like most desirable results, a glad heart seldom just
happens. The only free cheese is in the mousetrap.

We are never going to stop the rain by complaining, and a gloom-and-doom attitude is not going to
stop it, either. What will combat it is an unbroken
spirit and a happy heart.

We have it in our power to help the day to
break and the shadows to flee away.

How to Be Great

We don't have to be great to be great.
Anonymous

"That was a great meal!" "He is a great kid." "That was a great party!" "What a great afternoon!" We use the word *great* all the time to express deep satisfaction, whether it be in a person or an event.

Also, we tend to associate "great" with "famous," which is a mistake. Few of us will be famous. Few of us will occupy some post of outstanding leadership. But that doesn't mean greatness is denied us. A person is great who endures and is strong. He has great worth who sees a challenge as a mission possible in spite of a lifetime of toil, trouble, and tears. His life is also full of love and laughter.

All of us can be great in our later years if we really want to be. Now is the time to muster our strength, refuse defeat, stay active and interested. Then greatness will be ours.

We are like tea bags—we don't know our own strength until we get into hot water.

Freedom

Freedom is the right to do what you ought to do.

Bishop Fulton Sheen

Freedom isn't license, as we all know. We are not free to do things that would harm others. Case in point: no one is free to yell "fire" in a crowded theater.

The quote above is not exactly true if "freedom" is defined literally. The dictionary lists seventeen meanings! Here are a few: "civil liberty, political independence, personal liberty as opposed to slavery, not under physical restraint, absence of obligations." But the freedom Bishop Sheen wrote about is the dictionary definition that says, "the power of determining one's own actions." The quote needs to be paraphrased, however, by the words, "If one does not want to mess up . . ." because our freedom allows us to also do what we ought not to do.

The hope and the beauty is that we are free to choose to do what we ought to do, and therein lies our path to happiness.

Many times every day we have the freedom of choice in almost all aspects of our lives. Hopefully, we will exercise our right to do what we ought to do.

An Irish Blessing

May you always have work for your hands to do.
May your pocket hold always a coin or two.
May the sun shine bright on your window pane.
May the rainbow be certain to follow each rain.
May the hand of a friend always be near you.
And may God fill your heart with gladness to cheer
you.